My Old
Neighborhood
Remembered

My Old Neighborhood Remembered

A Memoir

AVERY CORMAN

BARRICADE BOOKS
FORT LEE, NEW JERSEY

Published by Barricade Books Inc.
2037 Lemoine Ave.
Fort Lee, NJ 07024

ISBN 978-1-62953-307-0

Manufactured in the United States of America

For my mother,
my sister, Jackie,
my Aunt Anne and Uncle Moses,
my cousins, Leo, Selma, Renee,
and the boyfriends who became husbands,
Norm, Cy, Lenny

PHOTO CREDITS

1. The Loew's Paradise Theater on the Grand Concourse south of 188th Street. *New York City Municipal Archives.*

2. The intersection of the Grand Concourse and Fordham Road. *Courtesy of The Bronx County Historical Society, New York City.*

3. Alexander's Department Store on the Grand Concourse and Fordham Road. *Courtesy of The Bronx County Historical Society, New York City.*

4. A World War II war bond drive on the Grand Concourse in 1942. *Photo copyright SofTech Consulting, Chappaqua, NY, USA and reproduced by agreement. All rights reserved.*

5. An eastbound trolley at the intersection of Fordham Road and the Grand Concourse. *Courtesy ouroldneighborhood.com.*

6. 175 Field Place, the building where the author lived, at the Grand Concourse between 183rd and 184th Streets. *New York City Municipal Archives.*

7. Newspaper photo of the Memorial Day Parade of 1946. One of the people looking out the window is the author. *© Daily News, L.P. (New York). Used with permission.*

8. The luxury area of the Grand Concourse. 930 Grand Concourse near 163rd Street. *The Museum of the City of New York/Art Resource, NY.*

9. The Concourse Plaza Hotel on the Grand Concourse at 161st Street. *Courtesy of The Bronx County Historical Society, New York City.*

10. P.S. 33 Elementary School on Jerome Avenue south of Fordham Road. *The Museum of the City of New York/Art Resource, NY.*

11. DeWitt Clinton High School on Mosholu Parkway. *Courtesy of The Bronx County Historical Society, New York City.*

12. Joseph Vitolo, Jr., the nine year old boy who claimed to have seen a vision of the Virgin Mary, praying before the crowd assembled in a vacant lot in 1945. *© Bettman/Corbis.*

13. The Ascot Theater and a partial view of the Concourse Center of Israel on the right on the Grand Concourse north of 183rd Street. *New York City Municipal Archives.*

14. J. S. Krum's on the Grand Concourse north of 188th Street. *New York City Municipal Archives.*

15. The uncaged lions behind a moat in the African Plains exhibit of the Bronx Zoo. *The Museum of the City of New York/Art Resource, NY.*

16. Joe DiMaggio at bat in Yankee Stadium in 1941. *© Bettman/Corbis.*

CONTENTS

This is about the Bronx of the 1940s and 1950s, my growing up years. I left the Bronx in February 1960. I was 24 and uncomfortable about still living at home at that age, although people still did so then. I was working in Manhattan and had been waiting to cobble together enough money to rent my own place downtown.

Her face and name are lost to time, but she offered me a catalytic moment. The young woman was from out of town and in my never-ending pursuit of low budget things to do on a date I managed to sell the idea that it was interesting to wander through the Central Park Zoo at night and see if any animals were out and about in their cages. We stopped in front of the polar bears and after watching them, we began to neck and then she said to me, "If you had your own apartment we could go there now." I was gone from the Bronx almost instantly.

I did not see her again. She went back to wherever she came from and I moved into an apartment in Manhattan. Much has been written about the changes in the Bronx from the 1960s on. When I left, the changes had not yet occurred in the part of the Bronx where I lived. I was among those who left simply because the aspiration of our parents' generation, to live in the Bronx, was not our aspiration.

Bronx neighborhood life in the 1940s and 1950s was similar to neighborhood life in Brooklyn, with similar demographics and similar iconic symbols of that life. The major differences I can discern related to size, in that Brooklyn being larger than the Bronx had more of everything, population, schools, private houses, and also more neighborhoods that were distinct in their characteristics from other Brooklyn neighborhoods. In the Bronx economic differences did exist between parts of the east Bronx and the west Bronx, still it seems to me more homogeneity existed among neighborhoods across the Bronx than was the case in Brooklyn, that growing up in one neighborhood in the Bronx was very much like growing up in another. But then I didn't come from Brooklyn and Brooklyn people might argue the point. Meaning no disrespect to Brooklyn or anywhere else, or anyone else's experience of the Bronx, this is what I remember.

175 FIELD PLACE

The building was a scruffy walkup with stores on the street
level. Our family's move there was traditional. We followed
the post-immigrant housing route which contributed to the
development of the Bronx of the 1940s—from low income
parts of the city like the lower east side to better housing in
the east Bronx and, for some, to better housing in the west
Bronx. We had come from a tenement building on Tiffany
Street in the east Bronx to this west Bronx three-bedroom
apartment on Field Place between 183rd and 184th Street,
an apartment with two rooms facing the Grand Concourse.
The ultimate in the Bronx was to live in a white brick, art
deco elevator building on the Grand Concourse. This was not
such a building.

A lifetime later I attended an alumni event of my high
school, DeWitt Clinton. I was a published author by then
and my name was announced as scheduled to attend. Several
people whom I had known in high school, who had remained
friendly with one another, decided to come. One of them
asked me, "Where did you live exactly?" "Field Place and

the Concourse." "Oh, the Concourse," was his response. "You must have been rich." "He wasn't," a classmate of mine dating back to elementary school said. "He lived in an apartment with his aunt and his uncle and a little brown dog." I placed my hand to my heart. I was married with children. Nobody in my new family held that as a reference to me, my aunt and my uncle and my childhood dog.

My aunt and uncle were deaf-mutes. They were the heads of household. One or another of my aunt and uncle's children also lived there from time to time. My mother, my older sister, and I lived as boarders in the apartment. My father had disappeared into another life before I was five and I was never to see him again. The move to the building from the east Bronx to the west Bronx was traditional. Nothing else about our family was.

In 1941, we moved into the building on Field Place. I can recall some shadowy images from the previous apartment on Tiffany Street. Other people also lived there. My sister, Jackie, older by six years, later told me they were boarders themselves. And I have fleeting shadows of memories of another apartment and perhaps the presence of someone who must have been my father, but I cannot say I really remember him or anything about him.

My mother, who was in all respects heroic, out of what was likely shame—it couldn't have been easy to have the only divorce in the neighborhood in those days, maybe one of the few in the Bronx—never got her story straight with me about my father until I was about twelve. Their divorce was made official by my father who filed papers in 1944, I eventually learned. The situation was similar to—as the writer, Lois Gould, once described—"a Jewish divorce." Defeated by The Depression, she said, some Jewish men, feeling disgraced for not being able to provide for their families, simply disappeared. Our situation was similar to that, but not exactly. My father apparently lost his job in the economic hard times, tried to operate a retail store and couldn't succeed, and having begun to pile up debts, fled New York. He stopped in the South and called my mother and asked her to come there with my sister and with me. My mother later explained she decided that if she joined him she would be always running and she declined. Her uncle, a successful small businessman, intervened. My aunt and uncle were asked to take us in, hence, the tenement building on Tiffany Street, and then Field Place.

When I was 26, I received a phone call from my father, the first time I had heard from him since he left. I was angry and the call went nowhere. Several years later, when I had become a father myself, I hired a private detective to find him. I wanted to get that phone call back. I thought now that I was a father we might have had something in common. I was told by an aunt who lived in Los Angeles and who once had known my father, that he was last seen somewhere in the Los Angeles area. With the help of the private detective, I learned he had worked as a bartender, had been living with a woman in El Monte in Los Angeles County, had used several aliases in his life, did not have any other children, and had died six years earlier.

People aware that I wrote the novel, *Kramer vs. Kramer*, and who assumed I must have been writing with emotion because of my own divorce were making the wrong assumption. I was never divorced. My sensitivity to the material was because my parents were divorced and I grew up never knowing my father.

ELEMENTARY SCHOOL

I attended elementary school P.S. 33 on Jerome Avenue near Fordham Road. When I think about the place it seems to have had its own underscoring, "Do you know the muffin man, the muffin man, the muffin man, do you know the muffin man that lives in Drury Lane?" which we sang and skipped to while a teacher played piano.

The school building was classic collegiate gothic, a slanted green roof with a courtyard, the design replicated in schools throughout the city. "Who do you think you'll get?" was the anxious question preceding each school year, the teachers running true to form, the same teachers there year after year, the strict ones, the nice ones, the mean ones, and as their reputations preceded them, so did they behave with few surprises.

We were at least thirty to a class, dutiful children. We carried fear along with our books. I can nearly summon that old knot in my stomach worrying I might be called on, worried I might be caught for doing something bad, and be told I was, heaven forbid, suspended.

The classrooms were hot and steamy in winter, the heat rattling through the radiators. As summer approached they were still hot, but clammy. You were obliged to bring a handkerchief and buy or make book covers for your books. The worry was your family would be quarantined if you got chicken pox, and you did get chicken pox, and they weren't quarantined.

At one point I was pulled out to attend a special class for stutterers, about six of us in the group who were told to read aloud to get our stuttering under control, an affliction that came as a surprise to me when I was told I was so afflicted. I might have stuttered, I can't remember. More likely I had too much to say in too much of a hurry. Or maybe not. After a while, I had done well enough to be excused from attending the class.

The school assemblies featured sturdy little children carrying flags in those days of heightened patriotism. Good George Washington was in full view in the auditorium in the ubiquitous reproduction of a Gilbert Stuart portrait.

Music appreciation was taught in groups in the auditorium as the phonograph played and we memorized, "This is the symphony that Schubert wrote and never finished . . ." We gathered leaves in the fall and they were labeled and placed on colored oak tag and taped to the class windows, the leaves gathered mainly from St. James Park, a fair-sized park located north of P.S. 33. I wrote a novel, *The Old Neighborhood*, and placed much of the action in that Kingsbridge Road neighborhood rather than my own because it fit the needs of the story. A woman, confusing fiction and nonfiction, wrote a letter to me and said she liked the book, but that she knew all the boys from the neighborhood and I must have changed my name for professional purposes.

We bought model airplane kits in a hobby shop near P.S. 33 owned by a Mr. Bess, American fighting planes, enemy planes. Some of the models required paper and thin sticks glued together and were rather elaborate, the balsa wood models easier for me. I was dreadful at this, even my balsa wood models were a mess, looking even worse when painted.

"Now write the numbers that you hear in the second column. Thur--ee, four." We were fearful of the hearing tests as we looked around the room when we could no longer hear numbers to see if anybody else was still writing.

Betty Suhr, will you forgive me? When I was sitting behind you, I stuck your pigtail in my inkwell.

Before ballpoint pens, the desks had inkwells and we dipped our wooden pens with metal pen points into the inkwells to write. We went through elementary school with ink stains on our fingers.

Oak tag, mucilage, deportment, fractions. Someone who was to always struggle with math in school, I am not thrilled to remember there came a day in elementary school when we started to learn fractions.

We were taught "tolerance" as to the beliefs or the nature of others. "Tolerance" was better than "intolerance," still, something short of "acceptance." To drive the point home we were shown repeatedly, *The House I Live In*, a short film with a message song starring Frank Sinatra. That would be the boyish bobby-soxers' Frank Sinatra, not the rakish Nelson Riddle Frank Sinatra.

Occasionally, my mother would arrange her lunch hour and take me to lunch at Thompson's Cafeteria near P.S. 33. This was a treat, to be taken out to eat lunch in a restaurant.

To the boys, the girls were not alien, they were like us with the same school experiences, the same fears, except they were girls. We played tag with them in the yard. They were our elementary school classmates, friends. Like Cecelia Klein who, when we were grownups, sent me a photocopy of the page I inscribed in her 6th grade graduation souvenir book, "Good luck ya dumb cluck." Then many of us went to all-boy and all-girl junior high and high schools and we were separated from a manageable social arrangement to a place of distance. I still haven't recovered.

I was in 3rd grade on June 6, 1944. We were released early from school to go to our respective houses of worship where D-Day services were being held to pray for the safe return of our fighting men in the invasion of Allied forces at Normandy. I went to a service at the Jacob H. Schiff Center near Fordham Road and joined with the other solemn children and adults in collective apprehension and hope. We 3rd graders didn't get adults to accompany us to those houses of worship. We just went by ourselves directly from school. These were our neighborhoods. We moved about them freely.

In 5th grade, our class drew an emotional bully as the teacher. She continually berated us for being stupid and sloppy in our habits and nowhere near the excellence of her daughter, close to our age, attending another school, whom she constantly held up to us. I hope things worked out for that girl. I did something really dumb one day and this teacher came down on me. When she wasn't looking I pocketed a ball she had taken away from one of my friends in the class and left on her desk. I seized it surreptitiously and gave it back to him. This is pure elementary school theatrics—the teacher told us she was going out of the room and the ball was to be returned to her desk in her absence, and if not, someone was going to get in serious trouble. I didn't like this teacher and I was tired of her bullying and I wasn't going to give in to her, not realizing in my 5th grade naivete that she knew I had snatched the ball.

She came back in, saw the ball was not there, walked directly to me and said I was the one and my mother was going to have to come to school. My mother come to school? My mother was working. My mother couldn't come to school.

It was agreed at home that for my conduct problem, my sister, who was a high school student, would come to school instead of my mother. And she did and it was embarrassing, the boys whistling at her as she came in, the fact that I couldn't even get a parent to show up. Well, that was in *my* mind. I was officially labeled a bad boy in the eyes of this teacher, on the road to suspension if I didn't mend my bad boy ways.

The teacher, let's call her Mrs. S____. We'll give her a break on the name. Mrs. S____ liked to repeat a story about a World War II soldier who had been in her class. He was told in battle, "heads down," and he put his head down because he learned in *her* class how to listen, and others didn't, and a bomb exploded and they were all killed, but he wasn't because, yes, he learned in *her* class how to listen.

I once attended the opening of a recreation center in St. James Park and addressed a group of P.S. 33 students who were brought there for the opening ceremony and I told them that I had attended their school long, long ago, and that I remembered having a really mean teacher. "Who? Who?" a couple of them called out. I declined to answer, but afterward a woman came up to me and said she was a teacher at P.S. 33 and had attended the school herself. "Was the teacher Mrs. S____?" "Yes," I answered. "I knew it!" she said. "She was so mean."

The mean ones, the strict ones, the nice ones were, by and large, career professionals. Many of our teachers came to teaching during The Depression. With the scarcity of jobs then, teaching was considered secure with decent pay. The approved occupation for intelligent women from the lower to middle class was to be a teacher. For intelligent men of their social class, for Jews and other minorities, corporate jobs were not available to *them*. Some of these men also gravitated to teaching. When we came through as school children in the 1940s and 1950s, they were there in place for us, these professionals—intelligent, conscientious people who might not have been teachers at a later time. Eventually, they phased out, they retired, people who became teachers because prejudice and economic conditions prevented them from being anything else. They were a unique generation of teachers. We children, not economically privileged, were privileged to be taught by them in in those schools.

Even with Mrs. S_____, when she passed us on to 6th grade, we were ready for 6th grade.

In 1997, I heard from Richard Kobliner, a former classmate and friend from the neighborhood, who had become a teacher himself in the New York City public schools system and was active in education circles. He somehow assembled a rough list of names and addresses of the P.S. 33 6th grade graduating class of June 1947, and a lunch was planned in a midtown Manhattan restaurant for the fiftieth anniversary of our graduation. He later explained some might have been confused and thought the reunion was just for our particular class, not the entire grade. Even at that, about thirty or so people came. A few brought their spouses. We were all in our early sixties. We were having difficulty trying to identify anyone, then when you looked at a name tag what clicked in was a face of a 6th grader.

We talked among ourselves and brought each other up to date as people always do at a reunion. Then we went around the room and we spoke to the group at large about something specific we remembered from the time when we were in school together. We probably hadn't thought about it in decades. I certainly hadn't. A theme emerged. We were children of the home front during World War II.

THE HOME FRONT

On December 7, 1941, I had just turned six years old and sat on the living room floor drawing primitive pictures of the bombing of Pearl Harbor to the best of my understanding. On September 2, 1945, when the Japanese formally surrendered, I was a couple of months shy of ten years old. In going from six to ten my range of comprehension evolved through these war years, as had that of my classmates, to a somewhat older child's sense of what it meant for the nation to be at war.

The war was embedded in our day to day life, the home front war all around us, the daily war news in the newspapers and on the radio, the weekly war reports in the newsreels, the shortages, the rationing, the posters, "Loose Lips Sink Ships," the people in uniform, the air raid wardens with their helmets and arm bands, the bunting in store windows, the parades along the Grand Concourse, the patriotism, the propaganda, the cartoon images of Hitler, Tojo, and Mussolini.

In front of the Loew's Paradise for a war bond drive, Liberty Bell Bridge was constructed and people who bought a bond could ascend the bridge and stand at a facsimile of the Liberty Bell and ring the bell for freedom. A captured Japanese two-man submarine was on display near Liberty Bell Bridge and people could look inside and observe how small the submarine was, which translated to how sneaky the enemy was. We were a nation at war, the Bronx was at war, our neighborhood, our block, our building, our families were at war.

With the war zones so distant, paradoxically the artificial depiction of the war in the movies made the war seem real. Bombs fell in the movies, guns were fired, blood was spilled, people died. These movies were usually simplistic, but then we were children. They worked on our children's minds in showing us that this war which so absorbed the grownups was being fought against a terrible enemy. We devoured the movies, *Wake Island, Guadalcanal Diary, Hitler's Children, Flying Tigers, Bataan, Winged Victory, Thirty Seconds Over Tokyo, The North Star, The Purple Heart, Sahara, The Fighting Seabees, Pride of the Marines*, and at the end of the war, as if to match in kind our getting older, we had the more nuanced, *The Story of G.I. Joe*.

As we grew older, our sense of the war changed from a vague feeling of menace to the sense of a real enemy who would kill you. We went from playing with toy soldiers and toy planes and toy battleships to making detailed drawings in our notebooks and in the margins of school papers and on loose sheets, drawings of planes and tanks and guns shooting. We were swimming in war fantasies.

At the 50th anniversary of our 6th grade graduation, one of our classmates said, "You looked around and suddenly all the men of a certain age were gone." In windows, banners with a blue star in a white field signified someone in uniform, and here and there a gold star for someone who had died. The Gold Star Mothers, respected, took their place in the Memorial Day parades.

Whether anything we children did genuinely mattered for what was called, "the war effort," I cannot be certain. Having all those earnest children involved with the war possibly contributed to the grownups' morale. It helped our morale. We bought Minutemen stamps and assiduously pasted them into books toward earning a War Bond. We joined in on the scrap paper drives. We saved Dixie Cup covers with action pictures of our fighting heroes. We were conscientious during the air raid drill blackouts making sure all the shades were pulled down tight, no air raid warden was going to shout, "Lights out!" at us. We wrote to our family members in service. The standard symbol of the home front was a framed picture of someone in service. In our family it was my cousin in his Army Air Force uniform and I wrote to him. It was my duty. We followed the football teams at West Point and Annapolis because they were Army and Navy. We understood shortages. Bubble gum was a scarce item and if we managed to buy a piece in a candy store we kept it for repeated use, storing it in a glass of water overnight like false teeth. We studied silhouettes of enemy aircraft, the Stuka, the Zero, the Messerschmitt, the Focke-Wulf, and would have been able to spot the invaders in the skies, no doubt about it, and call in the sighting to the police.

On V-E Day, May 8, 1945, with victory in Europe declared, we went crazy, throwing newspapers and toilet paper rolls off rooftops, the streets covered in a blizzard of paper, and we ran through it and kicked it around, a scene repeated on the day of victory over Japan, V-J Day, August 15, 1945. As paper fell on all sides in jubilation on V-J Day, I was on nearby

Creston Avenue and happened to see a gold star mother who lived there looking out her window. She emptied a small bag of carefully cut strips of paper, dropping the strips into the street. She watched the paper as the last of it fell to the ground and then she closed her window on the war.

MY AUNT AND UNCLE

My aunt and uncle would entertain other married deaf-mute couples who frequently came to the apartment to play cards. Their sign language was literal, not the style of signing you see on television and public events when someone is translating for the deaf. That modern style employs a considerable amount of shorthand, a gesture to substitute for a spelled out word. My aunt and uncle and their friends used some shorthand for certain common words, but everything else was indicated letter for letter, specific language, close to written language, as they spelled out the words with their fingers extremely rapidly. When the friends were together they were loud, they made sounds they couldn't hear, and they used broad facial gestures and every part of their bodies to express themselves, spelling out words emphatically. They communicated. They were geniuses at it.

An early memory is sitting with either my aunt or my uncle and playing a little sign language game. "I." You point to yourself. "Love." You hug yourself. "You." You point to the other person. "With." You place your fists together. "All." You roll your hands over each other. "My." You place your hand on your chest. "Heart." You place your hand on your heart.

My aunt and uncle's three children, Leo, Selma, Renee—and my mother, my sister, and I—all spoke sign language. I suspected my aunt felt embarrassed to be seen signing on the street. Her exchanges with me were unusually abrupt when we would meet in public. I picked up her embarrassment. I tended not to have prolonged conversations on the street with my aunt and uncle. My aunt had a limited command of guttural spoken language. My uncle could not produce language sounds. He was behind a wall of silence. In his concentrated, silent world, he had great patience for playing with children, as he did with me, as he had done with his own children. At his funeral my cousin, Leo, said, "He walked with the angels." My aunt, patient with me as well, was my after school card-playing, Chinese checkers chum.

Eventually, my cousins and my sister married and moved out, leaving the household consisting of my mother and me, and my aunt and uncle. My middle cousin, Selma, and her husband, Norman, who lived in the Bronx, were leaving to live in the suburbs. My aunt announced that she and my uncle were moving out to occupy Selma and Norman's apartment west of Jerome Avenue in the 170th Street area. I was surprised, but my mother was devastated. Over the years, she had contributed money to the household in increasing amounts, but it was my aunt and uncle's apartment. From the beginning we were, technically, boarders. The message my mother heard was that my aunt and uncle had been obliged to take us in when we were in need, but now with this other apartment available and my mother financially solvent, they could be free of us. My aunt and uncle may just have had the feeling they wanted their own apartment. My mother didn't regard it that way. "I thought we were a family," she said to me, disconsolate.

My aunt and uncle moved. I would still see them and they were present at family events. When I was going into the Army I went to tell them about it. The draft was in effect. I was approaching the time when I would be drafted and a couple of options were available to me, to serve in the Army for two years, and then I would have to be in the Reserves for three years, or take advantage of the newly created Reserve Forces Act, allowing me to enlist with an Army Reserve or National Guard unit, serve on active duty for six months and then attend weekly meetings for another six years. The comparisons seemed so complicated, the difference between the three years I would have to serve in the Reserves even if I had been on active duty for two years—versus the time I would have to serve if I went the Reserves route, that in trying to explain it to them, I took out a pen and drew a chart on a piece of paper. I was trying to show the differences and why I was choosing to enter through the Reserves. My aunt's face fell. Writing on a piece of paper was what speaking people, other people, did to make deaf-mutes understand. "You don't have to write it out," she signed to me. "We are not stupid." I had done what I had never done before with them. I wrote something out instead of signing. I felt terrible. I overcompensated with an animated conversation in sign language about anything I could think of.

I hope they forgave me. When my first child was born—they were still alive then—I brought him to the Bronx so they could see him. *The Old Neighborhood*, set largely in the

Bronx, is dedicated to my sons and to them—my uncle, who played with me with his infinite patience, my aunt, there for me when I came home from school while my mother was working—the people who taught me to sign. "I . . . love . . . you . . . with . . . all . . . my . . . heart."

A *TWILIGHT ZONE* TYPE
OF OCCURRENCE

A party was given in Los Angeles in 1981 in connection with the publication of *The Old Neighborhood* in a private room in a restaurant. Someone in charge of decorating the room for the party went into a photo archive looking for images that might have been relevant to the book and had them enlarged poster-size and placed on the walls. To get the full sense of this, one has to conceive of the odds against. An image chosen was from the May 31, 1946 edition of *The New York Daily News*, a view of that year's Memorial Day parade along the Grand Concourse. This was the first Memorial Day parade following the end of the war and it was a big parade with large crowds.

Out of all the various pictures in a photo archive, this was an image considered relevant to the novel and was chosen for display. The odds also strongly come into play against this particular composition for the picture, considering the march route was several miles long. The building that is in *the very forefront* of the image, the most prominently displayed building in the photograph, is my building, 175 Field Place, and if you looked closely through the halftone dots, you could see people looking out the window and since I watched all the parades from the window and would have been watching this parade, one of the people seen looking out the window had to be me.

Thirty-five years after the picture was taken I was looking at the picture which had been chosen to decorate a room for a party celebrating a novel I had written about my old neighborhood, the picture chosen out of any number of possibilities to represent that time and that place, and the picture included a trace of me as a little boy looking out the window.

THE TALKING DOG

I do not know if The Talking Dog was from the Bronx or only visiting. A crowd of children had gathered around the corner from my apartment near a man with a German shepherd and when I arrived the children were practically jumping up and down with excitement. This is going to sound like a child's imagination at work. Not so. It happened.

As I watched, the man said to the dog, "What do you want?" And the dog growled unmistakably, "Wanna hom-burger." "What?" the man said. "Hom-burger," the dog answered. To be accurate, the German shepherd spoke with a slight foreign accent.

He repeated the routine with the dog a couple of times and by then *I* was practically jumping up and down with excitement, too, and we were laughing and grabbing on to each other, barely able to control ourselves, never having seen or heard anything like it. The man then calmly walked away, discouraging us from following him and that would have been the entire story of The Talking Dog, except it's not.

About a week later I was listening to the radio, an amateur

hour show, Major Bowes or Ted Mack, something like that, and introduced was "The Talking Dog." The same man's voice was heard, "What do you want?" And the dog growled unmistakably, "Wanna hom-burger," with a slight foreign accent. "What?" the man said. "Hom-burger." And the audience applauded and that was the act. The Talking Dog, who was in my own neighborhood, and who appeared on the radio, was the first celebrity I ever saw.

OTHER DOGS

My childhood dog, Paddy, was a mixed breed with fox terrier lines predominating, your standard little brown dog. Sometimes a pure breed dog would be seen in the neighborhood. Honey-colored cocker spaniels were popular for a while. Most of the neighborhood dogs were part this and part that and if the owner didn't want to accept the idea that the dog they owned was a mutt, they said it was a spitz. The spitz might have been a specific breed of dog with specific characteristics, but not in the Bronx, not based on the wild diversity of dogs carrying that designation with owners who didn't know what their dog was and claimed it was a spitz.

Not many of my friends owned dogs and whatever else characterized my family life, I was given a dog. My aunt and uncle knew someone who couldn't keep this particular dog any longer and they and my mother signed off on the dog being taken in.

Lassie Come Home went straight to my heart, a movie about a boy and a dog. The movie prompted sidewalk conversation among us, "You know, Lassie is really played by a boy dog!"

Paddy was skilled at catching in his mouth pieces of cold cuts tossed to him in the air and we would put on a show on the sidewalk outside the delicatessen on 184th Street and Creston Avenue.

When everyone other than my mother and I moved out of the apartment on Field Place, Paddy now had his own room. The first bedroom when you entered the apartment was used as a storage room and in it was his dog bed. We would be sitting in the living room reading or watching television and each night at about ten, Paddy would get up from his position at our feet, he had put in his day, it was time for him to turn in, and he walked out of the living room and down the hallway to his own room and went to bed.

A prized dog of the children in the neighborhood was owned by the superintendent of a building on Creston Avenue. The dog looked part white labrador retriever and part something else, part spitz? The super spoke with a Polish accent and he called the dog, Vitey. We assumed the dog's name was Whitey, which came out Vitey. Either way, he was Vitey to the super and Vitey to us, and Vitey to Vitey. The man would say, "Vitey," followed by something that sounded like "sh-dai," and Vitey would sh-dai, he would sit. We found this to be marvelous, that the dog understood Polish, and we would say it and the man let us. We would say, "Vitey, sh-dai," and Vitey would sit. We clapped our hands, we congratulated each other. Vitey. He filled us with delight.

READING

Our literacy came to us courtesy of Dick and Jane and teachers who knew how to teach to the Dick and Jane books.

Odd to say it, the war was also an aid to our reading skills since we children followed the war in the newspapers.

Depending on the headlines, all of the large number of daily newspapers in New York City in the 1940s ended up in our apartment at some time or another, *The Bronx Home News, The Daily News, The Daily Mirror, The New York Post, The New York Times, The Herald Tribune, PM, The Journal American, The World-Telegram, The Sun,* which became *The World-Telegram & Sun.*

Comic books were also an aid to literacy. We had the highbrow comic books, *True Comics* with comic book depictions of real people and events: "He Bombed Tokyo, James Doolittle." "Houdini, the Man Who Mystified the World." *Classic Comics*, entire issues given over to one classic title, *The Count of Monte Cristo, The Hunchback of Notre Dame.* I was not thrilled about Archie, Betty and Veronica but they appeared in comics and I still read them. We were at war and we had

Captain Marvel, Sub-Mariner, and Wonder Woman to take on the enemy. The publishers of Superman sidestepped the dilemma created by his character—why doesn't Superman just end the war?—by having Superman a generally passive presence during the war.

We also read pulp fiction magazines and here I ignored the mainstays, detective pulp fiction and fantasy pulp fiction in favor of a sub-genre, sports pulp fiction.

Eventually, we made our way to the library to read real books. The brilliance of library systems, of guiding children along developmentally, was fully realized in our local branches. Story hour was a gorgeous custom, tykes crouched on the floor as a librarian read stories, the librarian lighting candles to mark the occasion of story hour with ceremony.

They should have kept the custom forever—to get your first library card you needed to stand before a librarian and read an oath aloud proclaiming you would abide by the rules of the library and take care of the books you borrowed.

When I was older I went by myself or with friends, the nearest library about a fifteen minute walk from our apartment. The walk gave the activity seriousness of purpose. You walked back with your arms full. I can only remember one title of a book I borrowed out of the many from my childhood library and it is obvious why I would remember that one. I had a dog and the title I remember is, *Lad: A Dog*, by Albert Payson Terhune.

STREET GAMES

We had the streets to ourselves for a while. We roller skated on the smooth, black asphalt with metal skates we clamped to our shoes and tightened with a skate key, and few of us could stop short; you slid on to a parked car. The asphalt was a perfect, dark surface to draw on with chalk, to draw pictures or play hangman, a word game where you tried to figure out a word your opponent chose and your wrong guesses were penalized and depicted by a chalk-drawn gallows which would hang you.

In the streets we had room to run and dart away in ring-o-levio, "one, two, three." Skelly was played with bottle caps flicked with your fingers along the asphalt. In Johnny-on-the-pony you would take a running start in the street and pile on a chain made by your friends' bodies. Jump rope was skipped on the sidewalks and in the streets, "A, my name is Alice, and my husband's name is Adam, we come from Albania, and we sell apples."

For off-the-point, a pink Spaldeen (made by Spalding, but never called a Spalding) was fired at the molding of a building so it ricocheted into the street, caught on a fly and you were out, bouncing once for a single, twice for a double, three times for a triple, up against the wall of the building across the street for a home run or caught off that wall for an out. Touch football with a real football or with newspapers rolled up and tied was played with blocking, and association football without blocking.

We were all over the streets with marbles when the marbles season arrived, suddenly, as if by decree. One day before, no marbles, the next day, marbles everywhere, our immies and purees and kabolas. The idea was to end the season with a big bag of marbles which we could admire for their beauty.

We would sit on the curb and at our feet we placed a box with cut-out holes and we would challenge all comers to roll their marbles into one of the holes from a fixed point in the street and we kept their marbles if they missed and paid off with a number of marbles if they shot it in the hole, depending on their distance from the box. In the high stakes version we would place a single marble between our legs and call out, "Hit the marble and get fifty" and from across the street the challengers would roll their marbles and try to hit yours. Freddy Krongold rolled a marble straight for the mark from across the street, hit my marble and wiped me out. I had marbles days of victory. In my marbles career that was a major defeat.

Punchball was usually a substitute for stickball when we didn't have a stickball stick or enough players. And we had stickball itself, the largest in scale of the street games, played with a bat that was once a broomstick or mopstick, cut to size from the hole in a manhole cover. Our version was where you self-hit the ball and ran the bases, a game that made us into borderline delinquents—windows could get broken—and the police broke up games, confiscating our bats which we tried to hide on running boards curbside when cars still had running boards.

A neighborhood baptism was to shout at the police, "You guys should be out chasing robbers," which you shouted just as you started running away, or an outfielder yelled, "Chickie the cops!" and the batter hid the stick and we pretended to be playing punchball with the outfielders a block away from home plate, a lame pretense since nobody could possibly punch a ball that far.

The superintendents of buildings were the enemies of stickball. The more aggressive of these supers nabbed our Spaldeens and punctured them with a pen knife.

In a good game with full sides of players stickball cut across age differences in our neighborhood, we kids played, older guys joined in, grown men. It was a beautiful street game. Even a lesser player could whack a ball and it would fly. Adults sometimes stood on the sidewalk or sat in folding chairs and watched us. Stickball could take up an entire city block, and why not?

Gas rationing was eliminated with the end of the war and the volume of cars moving through the streets increased dramatically. In our immediate neighborhood the main playing area was Creston Avenue along a two-block stretch. Other neighborhoods in the Bronx may have continued with a full range of games in the streets, not the case in our neighborhood. The heavily trafficked Grand Concourse was one short block away. Fordham Road and Jerome Avenue, also major streets, were nearby, so Creston Avenue drew collateral traffic. With the cars coming through in volume, we couldn't freely play games in the street any longer. We organized an occasional stickball game, but it had become too difficult to sustain.

Potsie, also called hopscotch, came out of the street onto the sidewalks, and that is where jump rope was now played exclusively, and with the lines in the sidewalk cement we played box ball, hit-the-penny, and curves. Curves involved digging your fingers into the Spaldeen and pitching it into a box in front of your opponent who tried to slap it into the box in front of you. If it bounced once it was a single, and so on.

We were busy on the sidewalks, we were not in the streets, although we were in our nearest schoolyard. Like farmers using terraced landscaping, we exploited all the possibilities of the adjacent schoolyard of the Bronx High School of Science on Creston Avenue. The space was small by schoolyard standards and was never used by the school or the Science students. It did have a basketball court and since it was right there, we all played a considerable amount of basketball, and occasionally punchball in the basketball area, and handball against a wall of the school building, and box ball against a wall of the yard, and in a narrow area behind the basketball court we managed pitching-in stickball, hitting out into the street. Displaced from the street, we used everything there.

In an early example of clubhouse politics, when the basketball pole in the Science schoolyard collapsed, one of the older fellows who was active in Democratic Party circles and who hired us to distribute campaign literature at election times, intervened and within days we had a new pole and backboard in the yard.

We scrambled over all the possible playing areas of the Science schoolyard and we played on the sidewalks, but the golden age of our street games, of children large and small in the street with chalk and marbles and jump ropes and Spaldeens and stickball bats had ended, overrun by Buicks and DeSotos like hippopotamuses in our midst.

CANDY AND THINGS

A major distinction between candy stores turned on two important elements, food and bookmakers. Some candy stores served food, mainly sandwiches. This distinguished them from those that did not. Some candy stores featured a resident bookmaker. This distinguished them from those that did not.

A luncheonette, as opposed to a candy store, concentrated on food and soda fountain items, but not candy store items. Candy store items were what made a candy store a candy store: Spaldeens, wax lips, Sen-Sen, Bromo-Seltzer, playing cards, Yo-yos, bubble gum, loose cigarettes, packaged cigarettes, chalk, jacks, baseball cards, compasses, button candy, wax bottles, marbles, packaged candy like Suchard chocolate, "say soo-shard," and Bonomo's Turkish Taffy, book covers, white paste in a jar, marshmallow twists, halvah, erasers, bottled sodas, marble-covered notebooks, pretzels, jawbreakers, pencils, candy in a tin cup with a tin spoon, licorice, pens, pen points, chocolate babies, loose-leaf hole reinforcements, jelly candy, batteries, rulers, cigars, paddle balls, gumdrops, razor blades, candy cigarettes, protractors, Dixie Cups, Pop-sicles, Fudgsicles, Mello-Rolls, coconut squares, harmonicas, comic books, coloring books, crayons, egg creams, malteds, lime rickeys, cherry Cokes, flavored sodas, ice cream sodas, frappes, sundaes, loose ice cream—a quart, a pint, a half pint, a gill—magazines, pulp fiction, newspapers.

Some candy stores had a wide enough storefront for an open window and signs with pictures of drinks and the prices, and a customer could stand on the sidewalk outside and sip drinks there.

The food counter in the five-and-ten also displayed pic-tures of drinks and food. The five-and-ten food counter was neither luncheonette nor candy store, but should be noted for the food art placed overhead on display, notably the Mona Lisa of the genre, the color picture of the hot turkey sandwich with a puddle of gravy sitting in the mashed potatoes.

Along with food, a major difference between candy stores were the bookmakers. They set up in either food or non-food candy stores, bookmakers being adaptable chaps. An indica-tion of a candy store with a bookmaker was a sign on the sidewalk outside the store advertising "Cars to the Track." If a bookmaker didn't hang out in such a place, and he probably did, then the horseplayers there could tell a person where to find one. Or a bookmaker might just be set up in his booth or on his stool at a conventional candy store working his book.

In a ritual for the horseplayers who wanted to see the early line for the next day's races, and for people looking to get a jump on the news, they would mill around the candy stores in the evening waiting for the first editions of *The News* and *The Mirror* to arrive.

Candy stores were as reliable as anything in our lives. They were open for long hours. Get up early in the morning, the newspapers were there. Need something at night from a candy store and there it was. In hot weather, for children it was our lifeline given the enormous amount of sodas and ice cream we required to get through life. Since candy stores bought their stock from the same suppliers, you weren't disappointed wherever you went, to your candy store or one that happened to be near where you were standing at that moment. You had something in mind, you bought it, you got exactly what you had in mind. Chocolate licorice was chocolate licorice. Some candy stores might have been lighter on the ice cream in an ice cream soda, more generous with their malteds, stingier with milk in an egg cream than others, but you weren't going to get a bad egg cream anywhere. Could there be a bad anything from a candy store fountain?

Sometimes we tried to be inventive, asking for different combinations of drinks, a chocolate Coke, a Coca-Cola ice cream soda, a vanilla egg cream. You were always looking for value, so Mission bottled sodas, containing a larger portion than bottles of Coke or Pepsi were appreciated, Mission orange a leading seller.

Naturally, people think their favorite candy store was the best. They were all the best. And mine was the best. This was Fisher's candy store in the street below our apartment. Fisher's was in the category of serving food with no bookmaker. Mr. Fisher featured an ice milk specialty, a "frozen malted." People came there for it specifically, which made Fisher's a rarity among neighborhood candy stores, a destination candy store.

In recalling candy stores of the past, some people cite the time before everyone had a telephone and customers would receive calls in a candy store and someone from the store would summon them. This is not a recollection of my days in the Bronx. We had phones in the apartments. A common memory is of the grumpy candy store owner harassing children who lingered over a comic book in the store without buying and the owner would chase them out of the store, not a recollection of mine either.

Because we lived in the building where the candy store was located, because they saw someone or other from our family on a regular basis, because I was a little boy who lived upstairs, for one, all, or none of these reasons, Mr. Fisher was lovely to me. I was given complete access to read comic books for as long as I wanted. When I was really little I would scrunch in a corner near the entrance of the store and when I was older I would sit in the rear and read away. A generous gift, to be able to read comic books to your heart's content from the entire array of comic books in a candy store. It made me feel like a rich kid.

GOING TO THE MOVIES

The Ace, Allerton, American, Apollo, Art, Ascot, Avalon, Bainbridge, Beach, Bedford, Boston Road, Boulevard, Bronx, Burnside, Casino, Castle Hill, Central, Chester, Circle, Concourse, Crest, Crotona, Dale, Dover, DeLuxe, Devon, Earl, Elsmere, Fairmont, Fenway, Fleetwood, Fordham, Franklin, Freeman, Globe, Grand, Interboro, Jerome, Kent, Kingsbridge, Laconia, Lido, Luxor, Marble Hill, Mount Eden, Metro, National, Ogden, Oxford, Palace, Paradise, Park, Park Plaza, Pelham, Pilgrim, President, Prospect, Rosedale, Ritz, Royal, Spooner, Square, Strand, Surrey, Tower, Tremont, Tuxedo, Valentine, Victory, Wakefield, Ward, Willis, Windsor, Vogue, Zenith, 167th Street, Whitestone Bridge Drive-In. Among others.

We went to the movies. Movie theaters were located on nearly every main shopping street. We saw everything. If we didn't catch it at first, we saw it later, or later than that. The Loew's Paradise and RKO Fordham usually showed movies soon after they made their openings in Manhattan. Then the movies worked their way into the neighborhoods in houses of descending sizes and ticket prices. Movies held on in the neighborhoods for weeks. This was double feature territory, B movies filling the slate, like *Boston Blackie's Chinese Venture* starring Chester Morris. When announcements were made for the Academy Awards, Best Picture nominees were shown as double features, as was the case in a pairing of 1954 Best Picture candidates, an unforgettable double feature I saw at the Loew's Grand, *Roman Holiday* and *Shane*.

Only when we reached dating age and certain proprieties were honored—you wanted to show you were appropriate and organized—did we bother to check the times of a movie to see it from the beginning. The common line while watching a movie was, "Did we come in here?" and if we really liked the movie we watched it to the end again.

In a vanished movie-going custom, if no seats were available, people would stand in the side aisles waiting for someone to leave and until then we watched the movie standing.

Going to the movies with family members was necessary, depending upon how old you were. Going to the movies with friends was excellent, except when we were of an age when we had to sit in the children's section presided over by matrons dressed in white and armed with flashlights to pick us out if we hummed through our candy boxes. Going to the movies when you were too old to get in at children's prices, but too young to be allowed to sit with the adults was a dark period in one's moviegoing life. Going to the movies on a date was also excellent, unless you ran into someone from your family, or friends who snickered.

Stories of adventures at the movies began to circulate in the neighborhood, the storyteller usually one of the local big shots, someone a little older, or one of the better ballplayers, and the main story line went something like this. The big shot went prowling the balcony of the Loew's Paradise on a Saturday afternoon, picked up a girl who was sitting there, started to neck, and felt her up. The story was always somehow about the balcony of the Loew's Paradise, not even the RKO Fordham or the Loew's Grand. This was a recurring story of the neighborhood big shots. Necking with a girl you picked up in the Loew's Paradise was astonishing to me, especially the feeling up part. Here's the thing. I believed those stories. And it never happened to me. Not that I tried. And I wouldn't have. Which is why *they* were the big shots.

The Loew's Paradise Theater opened in 1929, a fantasy palace, madly baroque in an Italianate style with a ceiling of stars in a sky of moving clouds. The Paradise was huge, 3,885 seats. A sold out showing of a popular movie meant a commensurate crowd filling the Great Hall lobby and into the outer lobby. This kind of crowd formed for *The Three Musketeers* in 1948 with Gene Kelly as d'Artagnan, Van Heflin as Athos, Gig Young as Porthos, Robert Coote as Aramis, and with June Allyson, Lana Turner, and Angela Lansbury.

The theater was designed by John Eberson, who specialized in these "atmospheric" movie palaces as they were called. His son, Drew Eberson, wrote, "I believe that even if we had the financing today we wouldn't be able to find the artisans who could create another Paradise." We in the Bronx thought it was unique. However, Loew's erected similar Eberson-designed movie palaces in New York: the Valencia in Queens, the Kings in Brooklyn, and the 175th Street in Manhattan. Well, it was unique to us, this elegant place in our very neighborhood.

The Ascot Theater, tiny by comparison, was a couple of blocks south of the Paradise and less than a block from our apartment. The Ascot was one of the first art movie houses in New York, the only art house in the Bronx. Classic foreign films played there virtually in repertory, *Beauty and the Beast*, the Marcel Pagnol *Fanny* trilogy, *The Baker's Wife*, and in the postwar period, the great Italian neo-realist films appeared in the Ascot immediately after they made their American debuts, *Paisan, Open City, The Bicycle Thief*. These movies that transformed cinema were not yet understood to be great and the theater manager would stand facing the audience as people exited after the first weekend showing of a movie like *Open City*, uncertain, asking, "So? Was it good? Did you like it?" And this was *Open City*.

For deaf-mutes, being able to read the titles on the bottom of the screen of a foreign film meant they could understand the movie word for word. So the Ascot was an extremely important movie theater for my aunt and uncle and for me since they took me along from the time I was small. Other members of the family had the Ascot in their reference and would go on their own or with my aunt and uncle and I would be included.

Children in the Bronx mainly went to the conventional movie houses. Because of my family, I went to the Ascot often. Later on when we were dating age, guys took girls to the Ascot to show they were different from run-of-the mill Bronx guys. I had been going there from the time I was a little boy.

In my life as a young man in Manhattan when The New Yorker and the Thalia on the upper west side were running vintage foreign films, I was interested to see those movies—again. I grew up on them.

SUMMERS

In the summer of 1943 our combined family rented a bungalow in Rockaway, the beach area of Queens near the Atlantic
Ocean. My aunt, my sister and I, and one of my cousins were
there full time, my mother, working in the Bronx, made a
partial commute arriving weekends, and my uncle, a clothes
presser in the garment center in Manhattan, came out more
frequently. We were in the Edgemere section near Far Rockaway. The war seemed closer at the ocean's edge. Lampposts
facing the water were painted black, theoretically to hinder
U-boats, and the beaches were regularly patrolled by military personnel.

So much seemed exotic my first time away from the Bronx,
the waves for bellywopping, the arcade games on the boardwalk, the silent movie house—an open air theater that
played Lon Chaney classics, *The Hunchback of Notre Dame*
and *The Phantom of the Opera,* the young men, some in uniform, and young women jitterbugging to a juke box on the
boardwalk, Takee-Cups—chow mein in a noodle dish; you
ate the chow mein, then you ate the dish.

Summers when we didn't rent a bungalow we were like all
Bronx families before air conditioning, we woke up sweating.
If you could, you went to Orchard Beach near City Island on
Long Island Sound. The good Robert Moses before he turned
bad, or the two sides may have been interchangeable, the
Robert Moses before he gave us the Cross Bronx Expressway,
built the Bronx a splendid beach and families went there as
often as possible. It was a tedious bus ride from where we
lived and a long wait to get out of there at the end of the day.
Still, most of us lived in apartment buildings, in hot apartments and we had a real beach to go to.

Children who carried towels rolled around bathing suits
were a common sight during the summers in the Bronx. Outdoor pools were run as commercial enterprises and charged
admission fees, a part of lost New York. Nearest to us was the
Cascades Pool on Jerome Avenue and 168th Street. Hand-
bills for Cascades appeared every summer in the windows of
retail stores. Bronx Beach and Pool was at East 177th Street
and Longstreet Avenue. At Crotona Park, 173rd Street and
Fulton Avenue, was a large municipal swimming pool. Sometimes people in the neighborhood went to Miramar Pool in
Manhattan on West 207th Street over the bridge from Fordham Road. I think of those places and I can smell the chlorine.

My mother began to earn a better wage and one summer
I was enrolled in the Castle Hill Day Camp. This was part of
the Castle Hill Beach Club, which competed with the Shorehaven Beach Club, both in the eastern reaches of the Bronx.
Shorehaven was larger and advertised "the largest saltwater
pool in the east."

We edged up economically and eventually my mother
bought a family membership for a summer at Shorehaven.
The facilities included the large pool, shuffleboard, volleyball,

ping-pong, paddleball, handball, tennis, basketball, tables for mah-jong, a sound stage with daytime and evening shows featuring singers and comics. A bus service offered a pickup point about a block away from our apartment and I went by myself when my mother was working or otherwise engaged.

The older teenagers and the older people seemed to love Shorehaven. At fourteen, I must have been too young for the place. None of my friends were members and I didn't make new friends easily. When I went to Shorehaven, even with all those activities, I kept to myself. Mostly, I swam in the pool and practiced shooting baskets. I just was never comfortable there. For others, Shorehaven was spirited with a pleasantly self-congratulatory air—isn't this great, aren't we lucky?—people of modest means happy about having their own club—in the Bronx.

THE BRONX HOME NEWS

BRONX SERGEANT IN AAF
MEETS HIS UNCLE IN ITALY

An Italian-American GI at war encountered his uncle still living in the old country. This headline from a story in *The Bronx Home News* of June 5, 1944, amid the vastness of World War II, is the newspaper going about its unintentionally humorous business, finding the Bronx in everything.

The newspaper came to our apartment each day. My aunt and uncle were avid readers and I became one, too. *The Bronx Home News* provided a child with straightforward, understandable reportage of the war with bold headlines and maps with black pincers indicating the lines of battle.

ALLIES PURSUE FLEEING NAZIS NORTH
OF ROME; FOE'S TENTH ARMY FACES
ANNIHILATION BATTLE

With its patriotic coverage, the war was not going to be lost in *The Bronx Home News*.

The newspaper was delivered to doorsteps and employment as a *Bronx Home News* delivery boy was a rite of passage for many Bronx youngsters. The newspaper was acquired by *The New York Post* in 1945 at a time when *The Bronx Home News* circulation exceeded 100,000. In 1948 it was merged with *The New York Post as The New York Post-Bronx Home News*, but was terminated soon after.

The lead story in the 1940s was usually coverage of the war or a story that might be reported in the other city newspapers. The rest of each issue was devoted to being the paper of record for Bronx births, deaths, engagements, marriages, for meetings of business and civic organizations, church socials, police blotter items, decorations of soldiers, block parties, war bond rallies, scrap paper drives, awards, appointments, school news, business news, news of local politics. If an event had a connection to the Bronx it found its way into the pages of *The Bronx Home News*. Advertisements ran for Bronx retail stores, Bronx restaurants, and Bronx businesses, advertisements that did not appear in other newspapers. These advertising pages were significant in conveying the sense of the Bronx as a place unto itself, our borough, and this was our newspaper, serving our borough.

In 1945, a nine year old Bronx boy, Joseph Vitolo Jr., claimed he saw the Virgin Mary in a vacant lot near the Grand Concourse. *The Bronx Home News* was out front on the story with the earliest coverage.

BOY'S STORY OF SEEING VISION OF VIRGIN DRAWS DEVOUT TO SPOT IN WEST BRONX

The front page article about the boy's contention was followed by additional pieces in the paper. Coverage in other newspapers followed and crowds gathered, increasing substantially, reaching an estimated 30,000. This was the ultimate *Bronx Home News* story, the Virgin Mary sighted in the Bronx.

ALEXANDER'S DEPARTMENT STORE

"Uptown it's Alexander's" proclaimed the store's advertising. Alexander's was located in each of the two important shopping areas of the Bronx. The first store opened in 1928 in The Hub, the East 149th Street transportation and retail store nexus, the second Alexander's opened in 1933 at the intersection of the Grand Concourse and Fordham Road.

At first, the Grand Concourse store was relatively ordinary looking with a restaurant at street level and awnings over the sidewalk windows. Awnings. Once upon a time in the Bronx, particularly along the Grand Concourse, buildings featured summer awnings over the windows. Announcement of a redesign was made in the fall of 1941 and the subsequent expansion and modernization resulted in a store that did not look like any other, certainly not like any other in the Bronx. Three long horizontal smoked glass window strips ran along the left and right facades of white brick. Vertical smoked glass strips ran down the center to the entrance. This was in the ocean liner style of architecture that came to dominate office parks.

The net effect within a retail area of no architectural style was that Alexander's looked ultra-modern and unique. A rendering of the distinctive exterior was used as a logo in the Alexander's advertising.

Along with Alexander's in the east Bronx Hub area were numerous retail stores including the Ludwig Baumann furniture store and Hearns department store, while the Fordham Road Alexander's was a flagship for the Concourse-Fordham area, which included Roger's department store, and retail stores east and west on Fordham Road and the adjacent streets of the Grand Concourse. These retail stores suggested the idea that the Bronx was self-contained, that people didn't have to go anywhere else for their purchases.

Alexander's offered the illusion of upscale shopping. It had department store size and variety and some fashionable items, but it was fundamentally a discount operation. With a working class clientele, which was the largest share of the population of the Bronx, this discount store with its modern architecture and promise of quality for value, was the perfect store for the Bronx.

My mother was a graduate of Morris High School in the Bronx and then she became the housekeeper for her several working older brothers. She married my father and through their marriage still had not yet held a formal job. When my father left, my mother, without money, with two children, her life in disarray, walked the few blocks from our apartment to Alexander's and applied for a job. This was 1941 and she was hired as a stock clerk for fourteen dollars a week. She became a salesgirl. A department manager. An assistant buyer working in children's clothing. It was postwar by then and simple blouses, sweaters, and skirts for girls were evolving into something new, children's sportswear, and Alexander's was selling it, and my mother was there for the start of it and she had an eye for it. She shuttled between the Alexander's store on the Grand Concourse and the store on Third Avenue.

J. W. Mays in downtown Brooklyn, another discount department store, was beginning to sell children's sportswear and my mother was hired as the children's sportswear buyer at J. W. Mays. Each day she traveled a long trip to and from Brooklyn on the D train and the A train. But she had become a buyer.

My mother had a long and successful career. She held other jobs after J. W. Mays, and died at 87 working nearly to the end of her life. My mother always credited the buyer who picked her out of the salesgirl line and gave her the promotions that helped launch her out of the working class. Anyone who might have cared is long gone now, but out of respect to my mother, and to that person, her name was Frances Simmons and the store was Alexander's.

ROOTING FOR BASEBALL TEAMS

The Yankees, logically, were our most popular team, but Giants fans were also sprinkled among us. The Giants' ballpark, the Polo Grounds, was only one subway stop away from Yankee Stadium and routinely we went to both Yankee games and to Giants games. Ebbets Field, in some mysterious place in Brooklyn, always seemed too far away. At the nearby Polo Grounds we could see the Dodgers and some of the outstanding National League players the Yankees didn't play against during the regular season, like Stan Musial and Ralph Kiner.

When a team with a star was coming in for a weekend series you felt the buzz among your friends on the street. Bob Feller pitching the Friday night opener for the Cleveland Indians or the Dodgers against the Giants for a series at the Polo Grounds—was anybody going? Going to a baseball game was not unlike going to the movies in that it wasn't a big deal, you just went. A typical moment: my sister and cousins decide to go to the Polo Grounds to see the Giants play the Cardinals and they gather me up—the little kid in the

house—and we all go to the ball game at the Polo Grounds.
We had more Yankee fans in that group than Giants fans.
The idea was merely to go to a game as entertainment. Both
ball parks were right there.

A separate thought within that. I was always being gathered up. I had no father. I *was* watched over. The people
around me, my mother, my aunt and uncle would take me
along to the movies, and my sister, my cousins, their boyfriends who became their husbands, would take me with
them when you might not necessarily take a child, such as
when they were going to a baseball game within their own
social lives.

I once saw a replica of the vanished Polo Grounds in the
Museum of the City of New York and what came back to me
was an olfactory memory, the way the damp Polo Grounds
corridors smelled of beer.

Youngsters my age were fortunate to be coming into the
peak of our baseball awareness at the very moment the game
was changed by Jackie Robinson joining the Dodgers for the
1947 season. Nobody I knew who was a Yankee fan rooted
against the Dodgers or the Giants. They were also New York
home teams, their ballplayers familiar to us. Only if they
were playing against the Yankees in the World Series did
you want them to lose. Jackie Robinson on the Dodgers didn't
mean we rooted against him, rather it was—why didn't we
get him? He was spectacular. The sight of Robinson running
from home to second on a double, or first to third on a single in
his choppy, rapid stride, and the way he tormented pitchers
with his leads off the bases was something you never forget.

My cousin, Leo, was the serviceman overseas I wrote to
during the war. Prior to his entering service he was looking
for a white collar job and anti-Semitism being what it was

in corporate life, rather than present himself as Leo Cohn, he changed his name to Leo Brody. After the war, Leo Brody found a job unusual for the times and for Bronx boys, Cohn or Brody. He became a motion picture publicist and worked for Eagle-Lion Films, the distributor of the 1950 movie, *The Jackie Robinson Story*, which starred Jackie Robinson playing himself. My cousin came to know Robinson as he shepherded him around for interviews and told me that one night they were walking along the street and somebody shouted angrily at Robinson after a game in which he did not do well at the plate, "What kind of hitting is that?" Jackie Robinson's response makes you wonder about the toll extracted for everything he gave. He died at only 53. He said to my cousin, "What do they want from me?"

In 1948, Satchel Paige, the long-time star of Negro baseball, became the oldest rookie in baseball history when he joined the Cleveland Indians at 42, an age that was disputed by some sportswriters as being too low. We were captivated by Satch and who wouldn't be, he was so colorful with his long, gangly motion on the mound. He made a significant contribution to the Indians, going 6 and 1 with a 2.48 ERA in 1948, helping the team win the American League pennant and ultimately the World Series. In our pitching-in stickball games we imitated Satchel Paige, trying to copy his Hesitation Pitch, a sweet moment in New York street games history, little white kids from the Bronx trying to be like Satchel Paige.

Two seasons after Jackie Robinson joined the Dodgers, their counterpart National League team in New York, the Giants, added two African-American players to their roster, Monte Irvin and Hank Thompson. Arrogant and stubborn in their racial prejudice, it took eight years after Jackie Robinson joined the Dodgers for the Yankees to integrate, one of the last major league ball clubs to sign an African-American ballplayer. Finally, in 1955, Elston Howard was added to the team.

I could not realize when I started out to be a Yankee fan how calcified the Yankees would be about race and class. Yankee Stadium sat at the southwest corner of the Bronx, removed from the rest of the borough. I cannot recall any outreach of the New York Yankees of those years into the community life of the Bronx. Not a single youth activity comes to mind for the area of the Bronx where I lived that bore a New York Yankees sponsorship. They were the imperial Yankees.

Radio broadcasts of baseball games were essential listening. At Orchard Beach you could wander along and hear from blanket to blanket on portable radios Mel Allen's voice calling a game. The very idea of a portable radio was somehow intriguing. It was portable, imagine. My pals would sit on the steps of the side door of the Bronx High School of Science, or another hang-out spot, the steps of the chapel behind the Concourse Center of Israel synagogue and listen to ball games. Except Richie Albert, who owned the one portable radio in our group, would turn it off during a tense at-bat saying he couldn't stand it and we would be apoplectic, but it was his radio.

Aided by ticker tape, radio broadcasts of road games were simulated in the studio. They were not a source of humor even with stilted sound effects to simulate the crack of the bat and roar of the crowd and long delays by the announcers as the tape came through. This was serious, interesting stuff, ball games coming to us from distant cities.

The nicknames: "The Yankee Clipper" and "Joe D.," "King

Kong" Keller, "Old Reliable" Tommy Henrich, "Tiny" Bon-
ham, "Spud" Chandler, "Scooter" Rizzuto. Lawrence Peter
Berra was never anything but "Yogi." I liked the name of one
Yankee opponent, the outfielder for the wartime Washington Senators, "Bingo" Binks, just for the sound of it. Because
of who he was, I also appreciated Ted Williams' nicknames,
"The Thumper," "Ted the Thump," "The Kid," "The Splendid
Splinter." We respected Ted Williams. When I was older, still
living in the Bronx, I took a trip through New England with
a friend from the neighborhood and we stopped in Boston and
went to Fenway Park. The Yankees weren't playing Boston.
We went there to see Ted Williams play, an homage from
a couple of Yankee fans to see Ted Williams in left field at
Fenway at the end of his career. He had been having a running spat with the sports writers and the fans. That day in
Fenway Park the Red Sox fans booed him. His playing career
interrupted twice for wartime service in two separate wars
and still he compiled gaudy statistics, likely the greatest hit-
ter of all time, booed in his own ball park. I don't think he was
ever booed in Yankee Stadium.

In 1946, lights were installed at Yankee Stadium and the
first night games were played. To market the idea of night
games the Yankees scheduled events before night games
were played. Yankee players competed against one another in
relaying the ball from the outfield to home plate, in running
the bases, hitting home runs. A klieg light similar to the ones
used to illuminate the ball park was set up at second base
and the catchers tried to hit it on a throw from home plate. I
went on one of those nights and it was baseball heaven.

Rooting for the Yankees allowed for many highlights and
then in a separate category was the 1949 season. To be thirteen and follow your team as Joe DiMaggio misses the first

couple of months of the schedule with his famous bone spur and returns to hit .346 the rest of the season, and for your team to go into the final two games of the season playing at home against the Red Sox, who are leading by one game and need only one of those two games to clinch the pennant, and for the Yankees to win both games, win the pennant, and then go on to beat the Dodgers in the World Series—I had an outstanding season in 1949.

JOE DIMAGGIO'S GLOVE

My mother handed me a baseball glove one night and told me it was Joe DiMaggio's glove. She was then a buyer and knew various children's clothing manufacturers and said one of the men she did business with was a personal friend of Joe DiMaggio's and gave her the glove when he learned she had a son. The best I can say about it was that it was an old, scuffed baseball glove. The glove did not bear an engraved Joe DiMaggio signature. It had not been autographed in ink by Joe DiMaggio. It was so well used you could barely make out the markings, but it was, according to the engraved signature, a Lyn Lary model. Now Lyn Lary had been a shortstop for the Yankees and a Lyn Lary glove was a fairly popular model, but I asked my mother why Joe DiMaggio would be using a Lyn Lary glove. The person who gave my mother the glove apparently anticipated my question because my mother said she had been informed by this man that the players didn't necessarily use the gloves they endorsed and that Joe DiMaggio liked that particular model. It sounded possible, not likely, but possible. I wasn't assertive enough to ask my mother to go back and get Joe DiMaggio's autograph on it or even Joe DiMaggio's autograph on a piece of paper.

The next day I took the glove and walked up the short street from our building to Creston Avenue where my friends congregated and I announced I had Joe DiMaggio's glove, that my mother knew somebody who was a personal friend of his and it was his old glove. The glove was examined and immediately someone declared it was a Lyn Lary glove, that it said Lyn Lary on it. I explained that the players didn't necessarily use the gloves they endorsed and Joe DiMaggio liked that model. Nobody was buying it. The unanimous verdict was I showed up with any old baseball glove. I kept the glove and I used it for punchball and stickball. Was it Joe DiMaggio's glove? Beats me. If a tree falls in the forest and no one is around to hear it, does it make a sound? If you have a glove that is supposed to be Joe DiMaggio's glove and you don't have proof of it and your friends don't believe it, is it Joe DiMaggio's glove?

PLAYING BASEBALL

We didn't play baseball, not in my neighborhood. My friends were such obsessed baseball fans, we followed our teams so intensely, so much of our street games had baseball in them, in the rules, in the fantasy aspects, they were street game versions *of* baseball, but actually playing baseball wasn't our experience. Boys who lived near parks in the Bronx with sandlot baseball fields, and there were a few such parks, might have had a different experience. Our neighborhood and the adjacent neighborhoods were dense with apartment buildings and retail stores and no baseball fields.

Creston Junior High School ran an intramural program, basketball indoors in the fall, softball in the schoolyard in the spring. Living right near the basketball court at the Bronx High School of Science we grew up with basketball skills and did well in basketball at Creston. We were also able to make the transition from stickball and punchball to softball in the Creston program and were passable softball players. We had no interest in playing baseball. With baseball you needed to be organized to play, nine players, hopefully, and another team to play against, and equipment. In Brooklyn, youngsters had the Parade Grounds League and Kiwanis-sponsored teams. We did not have a similar institutional presence organizing baseball for our neighborhood. And the older guys in the neighborhood from whom we took our cues didn't play baseball, so neither did we.

We were operating out of self protection—if you don't play, you lack the ability to do so, and we didn't play.

One time in an unusual occurrence a group of us went north to the baseball diamonds at Harris Field, located near Bedford Parkway. We were there to play a pickup game with some boys from that general area whom we knew. My pals were woeful on the field. Playing second base because it seemed right for my physique, I was also woeful. We never went back to a baseball diamond again.

One of the greatest ballplayers in the history of the game, Hall of Famer, Hank Greenberg, came from the Bronx and played for James Monroe High School in the Bronx. People of my generation were too young to have experienced his full greatness as a ballplayer. He began in baseball in the 1930s. During the war when our awareness of baseball was developing, he was in military service. He came to our notice dramatically when he returned to baseball for part of the 1945 season to lead the Detroit Tigers to a World Series victory. Hank Greenberg played until 1947. One of the major home run and RBI sluggers of baseball history—from the Bronx—from a nearby high school—Hank Greenberg couldn't inspire our hopelessly asphalt-locked group to play baseball.

EDGAR ALLAN POE

Poe wasn't from the Bronx, but he did live there, unlike Joe DiMaggio and Babe Ruth who only worked there. He lived in a cottage near Kingsbridge Road, historians tell us, from 1846 to 1849. While in the Bronx he wrote *Annabel Lee* and *The Bells*, giving the Bronx a nice poetic arc from Edgar Allan Poe's *Annabel Lee* to Dion DiMucci and Ernie Maresca's, *Runaround Sue*.

At P.S. 33 our teachers made sure we knew about Poe. *The Raven*, "Once upon a midnight dreary. . . . " with its mystery and rolling cadence was much appreciated. We were abundantly aware he had lived in the Bronx. He was our guy because a few blocks away from P.S. 33 stood Poe Cottage, his home in the Bronx. The cottage had been moved from across the street where it was first located and it had been restored. Open to the public, Poe Cottage contained furnishings Poe supposedly used, Poe marginalia and a bust of Poe. A small park on the Grand Concourse near Kingsbridge Road, Poe Park, was created as a setting for the cottage.

Poe's name was used for neighborhood businesses like the

Poe Garage and the Poe Raven Bar. Across the Grand Concourse from Poe Park was the best known bar in that part of the Bronx, Poe Cozy Nook. With the drinking age at 21, it was going to be a long time before I or any of my friends set foot in the place. We all knew about Poe Cozy Nook, a bar that promoted itself with wit. The matchbooks for the bar said, "Flat Beer. Rotten Food. Crummy Liquor. Lousy Service." Poe Cozy Nook was famous for its advertising; billboards in the nearby subway stations, a question mark leading into an all-type design filling the entire sheet, graphic design ahead of its time, text as the visual.

Poe Park was a narrow stretch with trees and benches, the cottage at the northern end and a bandstand in the center. Dances with big bands attracting large crowds were held in the park. At first I was too young to go to a dance in Poe Park and then when I was dance age, I wasn't socially adept enough to go, so dances at Poe Park were never part of my neighborhood life. But what would Edgar Allan Poe, historically regarded as dark and brooding, have thought of the idea that one day people would be jitterbugging outside his cottage? I suspect he would have been more comfortable with the idea that teachers would be teaching him and that local Bronx children would be captivated by his mysterious raven . . . and the bells.

"HAVE YOU GOT ANY INFORMATION?"

The phrase sounded like a line from a spy movie. By 5th grade we were wandering through office buildings in the Rockefeller Center area, making the rounds of foreign government trade offices accumulating "information"—promotional brochures for the foreign governments' commerce and exports. We would present ourselves at the receptionists' desks. "Have you got any information?" we would say and if we hit the jackpot, we would walk away with our winnings. Seldom did a building employee stop us from entering the elevators. We did not look like children up to no good. We looked like children there for "information." That is what we would say if we were ever stopped, "We're looking for information," and we were passed through. Everybody knew what "information" meant.

Latin America was a key focus of the brochure-gathering. We studied the culture and products of "our neighbors to the South." The Disney movies, *Saludos Amigos* and *The Three Caballeros* had been released during the war and Latin

America was in our consciousness and in the minds of curriculum planners and teachers in the New York City schools.

At the end of a period of study, the teachers would organize
culmination parties and show us products of the countries we
studied and sometimes introduce their food for us to taste,
like guava jelly from our friendly Latin American neighbor,
Mexico, which we declared was awful.

People from Brooklyn referred to going to Manhattan as
"going to the city." We said we were "going downtown." The
trip downtown on the subway was a direct ride on the D train
from our neighborhood to Rockefeller Center and most of the
trade offices were there. The excursion sometimes included
a stop at the Automat. It was intriguing to us how the com-
partments that were empty suddenly snapped shut and then
opened again and the food was ready, macaroni and cheese,
baked beans. Coming from a world of small apartment
houses and narrow candy stores, we were enthralled by the
skyscrapers, the offices, the Automat.

We were about eleven and twelve and not only moving
freely through the Bronx, we were traveling by ourselves
without adults to accompany us into midtown Manhattan,
making our way back, sometimes doing it solo. This was, no
doubt, also true of our peers in the other boroughs. Children
of the emerging suburbs enjoyed privileges we might have
envied, if only we knew better. But as city kids we didn't have
to be driven anywhere by adults. Independent, we got there
on our own. We got the "information."

RELIGIOUS OBSERVANCE

"The nuns hit." The Catholic boys in parochial schools told us that and used it as a proof of how tough they were. As we grew older, some of the Catholic boys studied daunting Latin in parochial school, which earned the respect of the Jewish boys.

Outsiders may have thought the Bronx then was primarily Jewish. I never assumed it was, not with so many Catholics in my neighborhood. The U.S. Census did not break down population by religion and the best available estimate then was a 1952 survey by HIP of Greater New York estimating nearly half the population of New York City was Catholic, about a quarter Jewish, and slightly less than a quarter Protestant. The Jewish population in the Bronx was undoubtedly proportionately higher than the citywide estimate and some neighborhoods in sections of the east Bronx may have been largely Jewish. Not where I lived. In the Concourse-Fordham area the sense we had was that we were in a half Catholic, half Jewish neighborhood.

Peter Decker, the former archivist for the The Bronx

County Historical Society, lived a few blocks north of my apartment on the northern side of Fordham Road. He has written that he estimated his neighborhood was 40% Jewish, 60% Christian, the Christians overwhelmingly Catholic.

With several Catholic churches, a Catholic university—Fordham University—the Catholic schools, St. Simon Stock and St. Nicholas of Tolentine in the neighborhood, and with the widely known Cardinal Hayes High School a bus ride away, the Concourse-Fordham area was a magnet for Catholics.

The Catholic presence, not only in the neighborhood, but in the city at large was always apparent to me. *The Daily News*, which came into the apartment every day, was intimately allied with the Catholic Church in a conservative political and cultural outlook. Francis Cardinal Spellman, Archbishop of New York, an outspoken conservative in church and non-church matters, was a major celebrity within its pages. Another luminary frequently featured in news stories—and this was the tabloid *Daily News*, crime was its beat—was the Catholic Manhattan District Attorney, Frank Hogan. The upper echelons of the Police Department and the Fire Department were dominated by Catholics and *The Daily News* was particularly thorough in covering Police and Fire Department officials and activities. The Catholic William O'Dwyer became Mayor of New York in 1946.

The most important Catholic in the world, Pope Pius XII, whom we saw in newsreels and in the newspapers, was so spiritual looking with his gaunt, solemn face, he seemed otherworldly and *very* religious. The Jews had no one who looked quite like him.

Some of the Catholics in the neighborhood went to church on Sundays. Given the large number of synagogues in the Bronx, some Jewish families must have been attending Sabbath services, as well. Not my family or the families of my friends.

Movies of the time, *The Song of Bernadette, The Bells of St. Mary's, Going My Way, The Miracle of the Bells*, with good priests and good nuns doing good deeds, contributed to the idea the Catholics had something going for them that we who were Jewish did not. We were not given *The Ten Commandments* with Charlton Heston as Moses until the mid-1950s.

In 1945, after Joseph Vitolo Jr. said he saw the Virgin Mary in a vacant lot a few subway stops north of where we lived, people began to hold a vigil for the Virgin Mary's return there. The devout, along with the ill seeking to be cured, came to pray and to be touched by the boy. Candles were lit, flowers were placed. Eighteen days after he first made his claim, the crowd coming to the site reached the estimated 30,000. For Jewish children of my age—I was nearly ten, about the same age as the boy—the situation was beyond our capacity to understand.

The boy did not have the vision again. A small shrine was erected facing the Grand Concourse after the crowds dissipated. The shrine was still in view when I traveled home on the bus from high school. It is there still.

The Catholic children who did not attend parochial school might have resented the fact that they had to go to school on days we were excused for a medley of Jewish holidays. I didn't even know what some of those holidays were for. What was Shemini Atzeret? And yet we were usually given two days off from school, the second day for the supposedly more religious among us. "Is it allowed?" was my standard question of my mother concerning these Jewish holidays. "Is it allowed to go to the movies?" "Is it allowed to play ball?" "Is it allowed if I play ball, but I don't run?" The rules for me became—no ball playing or movies on the High Holidays, but it was all right on the other Jewish holidays since we didn't celebrate them and my mother and my uncle went to work on those days and I figured my mother probably didn't know what they were either.

Although we didn't go to services, my mother sometimes slipped in for a memorial service on Yom Kippur. We did stroll along the Grand Concourse with the other Jews on the High Holidays. And we usually had a holiday meal to begin the important holidays. For Passover, we had matzo on the table and appropriate Jewish dishes, but it wasn't a seder, we didn't have a Haggadah. I had to dress "nice," for the High Holidays. By the second day of Rosh Hashanah, still excused from school, I was playing ball while dressed "nice."

For the Jewish children of my generation, our parents might have been able to speak Yiddish, and more likely their parents, but by our time, the language did not reach us, Yiddish overwhelmed by assimilation. The Yiddish language *Daily Forward* was sold at the candy store downstairs, tucked in a rack with other foreign language papers. Only a few copies of *The Forward* were ordered by the candy store each day. None of my neighborhood friends who were Jewish spoke or understood Yiddish and I did not. My aunt and uncle did not know Yiddish and never signed a Yiddish word. My mother, whose parents were Yiddish-speaking, said that she might have been able to follow a conversation in Yiddish and perhaps speak a little. She would not have had a reason to do so.

A teacher in 4th grade asked us if a second language was spoken in the house and barely any hands went up. In a sense, with sign language we spoke a second language in my house. I did not volunteer that information.

For Jewish children, Catholicism was mysterious. With

what little we knew of the Catholic faith, and we knew very little—our guides were Catholic children our age, hardly divinity experts—we could not track the ideas and the miracles behind the religion, lacking the belief or the knowledge.

This passed for a theological discussion on a street corner: A Catholic boy says that Catholics have a real religion and the Jews don't because the Messiah came to the Catholics and the Jews are still waiting for the Messiah. We have no rejoinder, not knowing how to answer. What is a Messiah and are we still waiting? The Catholic children were given the answers, we didn't have any.

"I have to go to Hebrew," were the words we spoke as we withdrew from a street game or left our friends hanging around. You had to go. It was decreed as part of your upbringing. A few days a week from when we were about ten years old until our bar mitzvahs at thirteen, with occasional Sunday School sessions, we went to "Hebrew."

My Hebrew School was part of the Concourse Center of Israel synagogue, a half block from the apartment. Bronx synagogues ranged from small buildings, which were converted private houses, to larger, more elegant synagogues built from the ground up, like Temple Adath Israel on the Grand Concourse where the Metropolitan Opera tenor Richard Tucker once had been the cantor.

The Concourse Center of Israel was one of the larger Bronx synagogues with substantial seating and a balcony. Identifying itself as a Conservative synagogue in the 1940s, the synagogue took a position that would have been considered Orthodox in later years—women and men were required to sit separately. I wouldn't have been aware of it. I never went into the synagogue. It wasn't a requirement for Hebrew school students to attend services and so I didn't go.

In Hebrew School we were not taught Hebrew as a language as we were to be taught French or Spanish in regular school. We were only taught to *say* Hebrew words. Pronunciation of the words was drilled into us. We read aloud. We wrote Hebrew letters and words in notebooks. That passed for Hebrew instruction because the principal intention was for us to stand up on the day of our bar mitzvahs and chant properly.

Our Hebrew School teachers, humorless, pinched men, older than our regular school teachers, suggested that God was looking down on us and observing our dedication to the task at hand, if you could believe that and I didn't. The instruction was strict, unrelenting, with a likely continuity to the yeshivas of Eastern Europe, except it wasn't Eastern Europe, it was the Bronx and seemed inappropriately rigid. In my Hebrew School we were moved around in the classrooms. If you answered incorrectly you were moved back and could move all the way to the last row, last seat in the room. If you answered correctly you moved up. Classes were held in a floor below the synagogue, sliding doors defining the separate classrooms. No girls. The concept of bat mitzvahs didn't exist in the neighborhood. If I close my eyes and think back on those classes in Hebrew School, I am tense, restless, and just getting over the chicken pox.

In Sunday School we were told tales from the Old Testament, the story of the Jews presented in dry reportage as if true. "Do you know what the word, history, means?" my teacher said. "*His* story." I found it all hard to believe and that was a crucial difference between me and the Catholic kids I knew. They seemed certain in their belief. They seemed to really believe the biblical stories they were taught.

The largest issue between Jewish and Catholic youngsters

was that we were told by our Catholic friends that the Jews killed Christ. The idea was passed on by the nuns who taught in the parochial schools of the 1940s, naive themselves in that era of backward thinking. It was understood by the Catholic kids that in biblical times our people did it. We killed Christ. The undercurrent from that thought never went away. In anything resembling a discussion of religion with our Catholic friends we were always off balance, lacking the information for refutation. We felt we were viewed negatively for this historic and monumental crime. In adult life I appeared on a television panel discussion with a priest from the Bronx of my childhood who said regretfully that the nuns *were* teaching in Catholic schools then that the Jews killed Christ.

We Jewish and Catholic children from the neighborhood when we were older and better informed might have discussed intelligently the known history of the life and death of Jesus and resolved the issue between us, but we were no longer there. We had scattered.

BARBER SHOPS

The barber shop was a reflection of the neighborhood as small town, our link with a Norman Rockwell image of American life. In the barber shops on a Saturday men would sometimes wait for up to an hour reading newspapers and magazines and chatting—politics, sports, complaints. They were in a man's domain, copies of Police Gazette strewn about.

For a child, being taken there by a grownup was not good. Being old enough to go by yourself, having been given the right amount of money for a haircut and tip, was also not good. The wait was excruciating. The talk in the barber shop had nothing to do with you and you could not possibly have an opinion the men or the barbers would listen to, even on something you knew about like sports.

When you were little you had to endure the embarrassment of being propped up on a booster board so the barber could get at you without straining his back. When you were older the barber cut your hair short for the summer, making this decision without your having a say in the matter. Eventually, you were old enough to have opinions about the way you wanted your hair cut and you asked for pomade and fussed about how your pompadour looked.

Like the shoe repair stores, barber shops were exclusively run by Italian-Americans. On a Saturday afternoon in the shoe repair stores and barber shops and through an open window here and there, the Texaco-sponsored radio broadcasts from the Metropolitan Opera House would follow you through the neighborhood.

A barber shop war broke out in our neighborhood. The barber shop I went to was located on the east side of the Grand Concourse between Field Place and 184th Street. My uncle went there and, therefore, so did I. The decor was basic, a narrow space with white walls and traditional barber shop furnishings. A contributing factor to the particularly long waits in this barber shop was that the barbers were older men and old-fashioned craftsmen, each scissor snip made deliberately, painstakingly, which translated into a haircut rendered very slowly.

In the early 1950s, a competing barber shop opened directly across the street on the west side of the Grand Concourse, nothing old-fashioned about it, black and white furnishings, slick floors, modern, and they used clippers extensively, and they got you out fast. The new barber shop was in the next building from mine. When I passed the shop I could gauge how long a wait I might have and I could duck in if they weren't busy, knowing I wouldn't be there for an interminable length of time as with the old barbers.

I switched over to the new barber shop. Many people did. Rumors circulated that the old barbers would go out of business. I wish I could say that craftsmanship won out, that the men in the neighborhood rebelled against fast and modern in favor of the deliberate, old ways. But the new barber shop caught on and was successful. The old barbers did manage to stay in business. Sufficient numbers of men appreciated them and were loyal.

As a teenager my hair was thick and wavy and couldn't get too long or the sides would curl up like the points of an elf's shoes. I failed to appreciate the care the old barbers took in dealing with me and making me look presentable. The new barber shop dealt with my hair by keeping it short on the sides, clipping away, rather like putting a bowl on my head. My pomade-reinforced pompadour on top served as a general distraction from the overall look.

I went to the new barber shop until I started college downtown and then had my hair cut in Manhattan. I never reached the age in the neighborhood where I was one of those men waiting, chatting, small-town style, in that old-fashioned barber shop. What I know now is the ritual of waiting was important to the men. And I know now those two old barbers were great.

GROCERIES, DELIS, BAKERIES, APPETIZING STORES

Several "Mom and Pop" grocery stores were located within walking distance of our apartment. These small stores were sometimes actually run by a husband and wife, justifying the "Mom and Pop" designation. Loyalty to your grocery was important. If you happened to buy something in one grocery store where they had an item your regular grocery didn't carry and you went into your regular store directly from there, you hid the bag so they wouldn't know.

The delis usually had a few tables for dining. Seldom did I or any of my friends sit and eat in our neighborhood deli. We ate grilled hot dogs, primarily, which you ate standing. Or I bought scrap pieces of deli for my dog and tossed them to him on the sidewalk, so it could be said Paddy also ate standing.

Sending us to the bakery for a rye bread was a dubious proposition for any adult who ordered up the bread. For most bakeries the goods were baked there, not shipped in. The bread was fresh, often recently out of the oven and it was the rare bread that arrived home via a child without one end or sometimes both ends of the loaf eaten.

The neighborhood appetizing store with its smoked fish and pickles—the store smelled of pickles—was a place my aunt particularly liked. We had smoked sturgeon and baked salmon routinely in the apartment the way other people had American cheese sliced and purchased by weight from the grocery.

This made for a rather bizarre experience for a child. My classmates were going to school with sandwiches for lunch—peanut butter and jelly, baloney, like that. My aunt made sandwiches for me to take that she would have made for herself. I was going to elementary school with smoked sturgeon sandwiches. Nobody traded with me.

ICE CREAM PARLORS

The most famous ice cream parlors in the Bronx were J. S. Krum's on the Grand Concourse near the Loew's Paradise, Addie Vallins near Yankee Stadium on 161st Street, and Jahn's near the intersection of Kingsbridge Road and Fordham Road.

Jahn's was a chain with locations predominantly in Queens and Long Island and was a late arrival at its Fordham area site. The place was known for its specialties like "The Kitchen Sink," a mélange meant to be shared by several people, but with its pretend Gay Nineties image, Jahn's was not popular among my family and friends. We preferred the traditional atmosphere of Krum's, and when we were near Yankee Stadium, Addie Vallins.

Krum's featured several outdoor signs announcing "Krum's Kitchen Fresh Kandies." The extensive candy counters with loose candy were a main feature of Krum's, "Over 300 varieties to choose from." With its extensive candy offerings, its large size, and its white-uniformed personnel, Krum's separated itself from the other ice cream parlors.

Various movie theaters were in the vicinity, making Krum's a popular after-movie venue. Because of the prestige of Krum's it was socially acceptable for adults and for young people on dates to go there even though you would sit at a counter and even stand behind people being served, waiting for seats to become vacant.

Krum's was where I had my first banana split, a slice of banana on either side of the dish framing a scoop of chocolate ice cream, a scoop of vanilla ice cream, and a scoop of strawberry ice cream, smothered with chocolate syrup, topped with whipped cream and a cherry. If I ate one today, I would feel guilty for days.

Of the 300 varieties of loose candy to choose from, my favorite was the chocolate covered orange peel. I would eat copious amounts of it, stopping only when I had pretty much reached the point of nausea.

THE TRUTH ABOUT MY FATHER

"If your father is dead, you have to be bar mitzvah-ed at twelve and not thirteen because you have to become a man earlier in the Jewish religion." That was what I told my mother, an interesting piece of apocryphal information. I was then approaching twelve, which would have made my bar mitzvah imminent. I was working a strategy to unearth the truth about my father.

No family photographs existed of my father, alone or with my mother, or my sister, or with me. He was never discussed. No reference was made about him to fix moments of our life in time. I had been told he was dead. First, he supposedly died in the war in the Canadian Army. We had Canadian relatives, a cousin of mine was in the Canadian Army, and I must have asked where my father was and when my mother told me my father died, I must have followed up by asking if he died in the war in the Canadian Army and my mother, overwhelmed by her situation, probably said he did.

As I got a little older, my mother either changed or lost track of the story line and my father had died in a car crash.

As an adult when I returned to P.S. 33 to address the children at an assembly, I was given as a gift a copy of my elementary school record which began in September 1941 when my mother enrolled me in 1st grade. Next to my father's name it said, "Deceased." So I wasn't the only one she was telling tales to.

My father was like someone who had never lived. This might not have been the case had I been able to confront my mother and ask what was the truth, or confront my older sister. I was complicit with the silence. Until I wasn't. Scheming, I made up a story for my aunt, my pal in playing cards after school, and I said some boys teased me about not having a father. Completely untrue. "Do you want to know where your father is?" she asked me, signing. I nodded that I would. "California," she said. She was often puckish and was so as she told me this, letting me in on something between us. "Don't tell anybody I told you." "I promise," I said.

California. The shifting stories about how my father died now made sense. The stories shifted because they weren't true. I couldn't break faith with my aunt and implicate her. And that was when I came up with my idea of flushing out the truth by rewriting the bar mitzvah requirements and confronting my mother with the complications therein.

She did not respond immediately. A few days later, I was told to come into the living room and my mother and sister sat across from me, both with grave expressions. My mother began elsewhere, telling me about my cousin's boyfriend. My cousin, Renee, with whom we lived, was about eighteen at the time and going with a young man who believed, because that was what he had been told, that his mother was dead. He had just found out his mother was not dead, she was alive and in a mental institution. The young man was deeply upset and my mother said she had decided she didn't want me to be similarly upset some time in the future to discover what I had been told about my father wasn't true. My father was alive. My father and mother were divorced. He had abandoned his family before my fifth birthday and when my sister was almost twelve. He had run out on us, deserted us, my mother said. He had made no attempt to be in touch with us or send money and he had left us to move in with relatives. He hadn't sent letters or birthday cards to his children. He had no interest in us. "I told you he was dead because he's as good as dead," my mother said. He once was a salesman for a paper company, she told me, but he couldn't hold on to the job. My mother's uncle set him up in a shoe store, but he couldn't run it properly and the business went under. She said he was a bad man. He gambled. He had debts. My mother had been paying off some of his debts to a collection agency, a few dollars a month. The collection agency representative agreed to that because he said it was taking milk from babies. She was still paying every month. If my father cared about me or my sister we would have heard from him and we had not.

Some of this, revealed in another conversation a few years later, turned out not to be strictly true. My father did leave New York, trailing debts behind. But he did call my mother from somewhere in the South some days afterward and asked her to meet him and bring the children. Making a stand, my mother refused to do so. So it was not exactly abandonment. Thorough editing in this first revelation was not being done by mother, who was going for, what became known in our school studies, as The Main Theme.

And then my mother added an additional piece of information about my father that was to have a lingering effect on my sense of self and my feelings about my background. She told me he had held up a candy store and was caught. My mother said she received a call to come down to a police station and at the station was a husband and wife who owned the candy store and my father was there. My mother said she got on her knees, crying, begging the couple not to press charges, that she had young children at home and couldn't have their father in jail and they took pity on her and my father was released. So many questions arose about that incident, including the desperate state of mind he must have been in if the story were true, but the questions didn't occur to me until I was older. What I came away with was that I had a father who was a bad man who didn't love his children or he wouldn't have run off, and didn't even send us birthday cards, so bad a man that he held up a candy store. My mother concluded by saying that when she went out to work it wouldn't have looked good if she had said her husband had left her, so she told people her husband was dead. And that was what I was to say if anybody asked. He was dead. That was all anyone had to know.

You side with the parent who stays and such was my loyalty that for a few years I did maintain my father was dead. That broke open when I was about seventeen and my first real girlfriend asked me what was the saddest thing that ever happened to me. I told her when I had to bring my dog, Paddy, to the vet to be put down, and she looked at me oddly, and I knew somehow she was aware that my parents were divorced and knew I was lying, that it may have been common knowledge in the neighborhood, or she didn't know at all and just thought I was simply a total jerk for not saying the saddest thing was when my father died, which I couldn't say because he hadn't. I went home and told my mother I had lied for her that night, but was never going to lie for her again.

When my mother told me about my father she said she had

learned you weren't bar mitzvah-ed at twelve, as I claimed. It was thirteen, regardless. So we were back to normal on that particular front.

Periodically, music teachers who made the rounds of Hebrew schools would come to teach us songs to commemorate holidays, songs like *I Have a Little Dreidel* and *Rock of Ages*. The music teacher at the Concourse Center of Israel was one of these roving music teachers. He was younger than our teachers, possibly in his thirties. We liked the singing, a break from the tedium. One afternoon when we were finished, he asked me to stay. He took me upstairs to the synagogue portion of the building to an alcove where there was a piano. He played a note and asked me to reproduce the note by humming it. I did and he repeated the procedure with several notes on the piano as I hummed accordingly. Then he said he wanted to see if I could sing in Hebrew and he played something I had never heard before and sang the accompanying Hebrew words. He played and sang a few times, then asked me to sing it with him and I did, as he corrected me. After a few minutes of this he told me I had a very good voice and I could reproduce notes I heard on the piano and he wanted me to be in a professional choir of his, that it was older men and some boys and they sang at weddings and bar mitzvahs and wore robes and it was a very special thing to do and if I did it I would also be paid. I was to speak with my parents at home. He would be back and we would discuss it further.

All that about my father. And now this. Everything was too complicated. And I hated Hebrew School. I wanted no part of singing in a choir. I took the siddur, the prayer book our Hebrew School teacher said was holy and I took my other Hebrew School books and I threw everything down the incinerator.

Then I started playing hooky from Hebrew School. Nobody played hooky from Hebrew School. It would be a sin. But then you had to believe in something about it to believe it was a sin and I didn't believe in anything about it, not God, not the biblical stories. I played basketball when I was supposed to be in Hebrew School, I took walks, I passed the time. My mother was working, she didn't know my whereabouts. My aunt couldn't tell I was not going to Hebrew School. I often went there without coming home first. I can't imagine what I was thinking with my fevered little brain, how long I thought I could get away with it before I was caught, what the outcome could be.

After three weeks or so, somebody called the apartment from the Hebrew School office and asked what was going on, that I hadn't been attending classes. My mother, furious, summoned me for an explanation. I said I didn't want to go to Hebrew School anymore. Every Jewish boy in the Bronx went to Hebrew School and was bar mitzvah-ed. I was confronting her with a cultural impossibility. Given the recent revelation about my father and the rebellious child before her, she made a choice. She said I didn't have to go, at least not immediately, but further down the road as it came closer to the assigned date for my bar mitzvah I would have to go back and finish up. They had told her at the school that I was a good student, which meant I would be able to return with enough time remaining to learn what I needed to learn for my bar mitzvah. I made the deal.

I didn't attend Hebrew School for the next six months or so and then as the time came closer to my bar mitzvah date, scheduled for December 1948, I returned—with one slight problem. In the time I was away, and as part of my rebellion, I could no longer identify the letters in Hebrew. I had forgotten everything. I wasn't pretending. It was all a blank to me.

My mother must have engaged in some behind the scenes discussions because I was told the son of my Hebrew School teacher, a young man who sometimes tutored Hebrew, would tutor me in what I needed to know so that I could chant properly on the day of my bar mitzvah. I relearned enough to manage the words and the chanting.

Another boy was bar mitzvah-ed along with me. In front of the congregation the rabbi took a few moments to acknowledge the other boy. The teachers spoke to us in Hebrew School about "going on," continuing Hebrew studies after the bar mitzvah. This other boy, who had reprimanded me for opening a telegram given to me during the service, saying, "You don't tear paper in the synagogue!" he was "going on," the rabbi proudly announced. I was not.

A small reception after the service was held in the basement of the synagogue where the Hebrew School classes met. I gave a short speech for the guests consisting of family members, among them a couple of uncles I barely knew—my mother's brothers who did not have a presence in my life—and some of my mother's business associates. My sister, who through my entire life was a supporter of mine, wrote the speech for me. As for the service in the synagogue, I did it. I performed what I needed to chant. I got through it.

I did not set foot in a synagogue for another twenty-three years. Rabbi Gunter Hirschberg of Temple Rodeph Sholom on the upper west side of Manhattan invited me to attend a Friday night service to hear a sermon he was delivering on the subject of my novel, *Oh, God!* and I attended. Inevitably, I thought back to my last time in a synagogue, to my bar mitzvah day, when I was like an ailing child prince propped up to wave at the populace.

TELEVISION

The crowd gathered in front of the store window and I considered myself lucky to squeeze into a space with a clear view of the screen for the Joe Louis-Jersey Joe Walcott heavyweight championship fight from Yankee Stadium in June 1948. Television had arrived in the Bronx, not yet in our apartment or in the apartments of the people I knew, on view through the windows of the television sales and repair shops beginning to appear throughout the Bronx. The store owners closed their doors at night, left a television set turned on in the window and let the set play and do the business of selling the idea of television. Not much selling was required. Within a couple of years or so of that fight everyone I knew, including my family, owned a television set.

Previously, for home entertainment we had phonograph records, 78s my sister and cousin brought home like Tony Pastor's *One Meat Ball*, said meat ball which you "gets no bread with," and albums like *Ballad for Americans*, sung by Paul Robeson. And we had beloved radio—the war news, the sports events, the comedy shows, Jack Benny, Fred Allen,

Bob Hope, Edgar Bergen and Charlie McCarthy—a ventrilo-
quist on the radio—our programs, *Tennessee Jed, The Lone
Ranger*, the dramas, *Lights Out* and *Escape*. But with television suddenly we had riveting visual images and the television sets were headed right for our living rooms.

Television went into our living rooms because that is
where our console radios had been and television was so
extraordinary, placement in a living room where we could
gather around was demanded. Some people were concerned
about how a television set was to be integrated into the living room decor. The standard look of the furnishings in the
Bronx apartments I knew relied heavily on mahogany pieces
for status. Consequently, many of the early television sets in
the Bronx were in the talking furniture category, inserted
in cabinetry which was often made of mahogany with cabi-
net doors that closed on the screen so when the set was not
turned on it looked like a piece of living room furniture.
Sort of.

A store near our apartment specialized in this kind of dis-
guised television set and that was the kind we ended up with,
cabinetry containing an off-brand television set that went on
to live a sickly life requiring constant repairs within its fancy
trappings.

A new social arrangement came out of these early days of
television ownership, the visiting of friends or relatives who
owned a set. My brother-in-law's cousins owned one of the
first television sets and this was an event, going over to their
apartment and I went one evening with my sister, brother-in-
law, and my mother. It was important enough for my mother
to wear a new black dress, something I especially remember because one of the cousins present, my mother's age, was
wearing the identical black dress causing embarrassment for

The Loew's Paradise Theater on the Grand Concourse south of 188th Street.

The intersection of the Grand Concourse and Fordham Road.

Alexander's Department Store on the Grand Concourse and Fordham Road.

A World War II war bond drive on the Grand Concourse in 1942.

An eastbound trolley at the intersection of Fordham Road and the Grand Concourse.

175 Field Place, the building where the author lived, at the Grand Concourse between 183rd and 184th Streets.

Newspaper photo of the Memorial Day Parade of 1946. One of the people looking out the window is the author.

The luxury area of the Grand Concourse. 930 Grand Concourse near 163rd Street.

The Concourse Plaza Hotel on the Grand Concourse at 161st Street.

P.S. 33 Elementary School on Jerome Avenue south of Fordham Road.

DeWitt Clinton High School on Mosholu Parkway.

Joseph Vitolo, Jr., the nine year old boy who claimed to have seen a vision of the Virgin Mary, praying before the crowd assembled in a vacant lot in 1945.

The Ascot Theater and a partial view of the Concourse Center of Israel on the right on the Grand Concourse north of 183rd Street.

J. S. Krum's on the Grand Concourse north of 188th Street.

The uncaged lions behind a moat in the African Plains exhibit of the Bronx Zoo.

Joe DiMaggio at bat in Yankee Stadium in 1941.

them both. Significant about the incident was that the evening, gathering in someone's apartment to watch television, was considered dress-up by the women.

The first friend of mine to own a television set was my classmate from junior high school, Ben Miller. A relative of his built a television set for Ben's family from an electronics kit. Heady stuff to someone like me who had been inept in making model airplanes. In an exclusive boys' clubhouse activity, Ben would invite friends to watch Milton Berle.

When we owned our own television set I was so thrilled I watched anything, even Jon Gnagy demonstrating how to draw pictures I wouldn't dream of emulating and didn't try.

Since each television set required a separate roof antenna, competition became intense for rooftop space to accommodate the antennas which altered the skyline. Antenna wires flopped over the roofline into the various apartments. We pointed out our antennas to our friends as though we owned real estate.

The reception in the Bronx was shaky, nobody in our area was able to get a clear image of the Dumont Television Network, which came in with a shadowy ghost. And the sets were shoddy, tubes were constantly burning out. Men who had been fix-it guys with radio repair shops were now television repair experts, nearly as important as doctors who made house calls.

In deciding whether to see a movie without subtitles, my aunt and uncle would ask, "Is there a lot of talking?" If not a lot of talking, they would go to a movie theater to see the movie. Accordingly, they watched television with the rest of us when there was not a lot of talking, as with variety shows.

The Brooklyn Dodgers were the best team to watch on television. They featured more advanced television coverage than the Yankees and the Giants. The Dodgers had their Zoomar close-up cameras installed in the dugouts at Ebbets Field—Don Newcombe, focused and perspiring, staring in from the mound. Yankee fans watched Dodgers games just for the coverage.

One day we found ourselves looking wide-eyed at television through store windows and in a dramatically short period of time television was part of our lives. As the industry figured out the medium, the programming was scattered, ranging from the live dramas, *Studio One* and *Kraft Television Theater* to roller derby and wrestling. Teenagers caught up in the magic, we passed along the hearsay that the wrestler, Antonino Rocca, was so fierce that in Argentina he killed a man in the ring, which we believed just as we believed Antonino Rocca's wrestling matches were on the level.

SCHOOLYARD BASKETBALL

Schoolyard basketball was played continuously, on scorching summer days and on courts cleared of snow, played by day and by night with the light of lampposts, played by dirty ballplayers who could never foul out because nobody kept track of fouls, and crybabies who would cry foul if you grazed their shirts, played between stellar ballplayers and hapless ballplayers, between goody-two-shoes students and academic ne-er do-wells. Democracy in action.

Every neighborhood had its schoolyard basketball standouts, some who went on to play for high school and college teams and sometimes returned to play in the schoolyards where it all began for them.

If anybody bothered to calculate, many of us probably spent more time playing schoolyard basketball than any other activity, apart from physically sitting in a classroom.

The world contained in a schoolyard basketball court was compressed, intense, something the boys did that the girls did not. You never saw girls playing schoolyard basketball. The basic form was the three-man game. Every once in a while a full-court game was played. Winners stayed on, losers got off. If you lost, it wasn't a crushing defeat. You might have to wait your turn to play again. If you won, you won court time, like with a pinball machine.

Which neighborhood had the best basketball players was impossible to determine. Good ballplayers came out of every neighborhood and some went on to have well-regarded basketball careers. Where I lived we had the advantage of the small-scale court in the Bronx High School of Science schoolyard to learn our skills before moving up to the Creston Junior High schoolyard. Madison Square Garden was referred to in the sports pages as "the Mecca of college basketball." The Mecca of schoolyard basketball in our part of the Bronx was the schoolyard at Creston. With the active intramural basketball program at the school, you were caught up in the basketball-mindedness of the place. You played on the Creston schoolyard court whenever you could and when you went on to high school you still played there.

In my time important ballplayers could be seen on the court at Creston, Dolph Schayes, who starred for DeWitt Clinton High School, N.Y.U., and the Syracuse Nationals of the NBA and who would be named to the NBA Hall of Fame, Jack Molinas, who led Columbia to an Ivy League championship and who was a story unto himself, Arnie Stein, who played with Dayton University in the NIT Tournament, Bobby Santini, who played for Iona College, Ed Roman from the C.C.N.Y. double championship team, Dick Kor of N.Y.U., Danny Lyons of Fordham University. When any of these players were on the court, a crowd formed on the sidelines and behind the schoolyard fence, neighborhood people watching neighborhood people who were, unquestionably in our minds, stars.

JUNIOR HIGH SCHOOL

We moved on from Mrs. S_____ in 5th grade to Mr. Katz in 6th grade, a man who comported himself with personal dignity and who was courteous to us. We were taught, we paid attention, the school year passed without drama. We were headed for junior high school and the great divide, boys to Creston Junior High School, girls to Elizabeth Barrett Browning Junior High School.

They assigned me to the "SPs" for junior high school. For years in the New York City public schools some students were designated for classes called, variously, the "Rs" and the "RAs." These supposedly more capable students went through an accelerated course of study in junior high school and skipped a grade. When it was our turn to enter junior high, the nomenclature had been changed and the rapid advance classes were to be called "special progress classes," "SPs." Why some students were selected rather than others, what the standards were, never was explained to us. Tracking children at twelve or thirteen had to be hit or miss. Whatever the selection process, it could not assess students with skills not easily observed, or students who developed late, or those going through a difficult time for any number of external reasons. Surely an enormous number of students over the years who were not identified for the minor distinction of skipping a grade in junior high school went on to live meritorious lives.

I don't know on what basis I was assigned. Maybe I had good reading skills—from an early start reading titles of foreign movies at the Ascot perhaps? But in junior high the first serious signs of deficiencies on my part in math began to show up and they followed me right through junior high and high school like the rain cloud over the head of Joe Btfsplk in the *Li'l Abner* comic strip.

At Creston, unlike elementary school, we moved period by period to other teachers and other subjects. Some classes seemed to be holdovers from The Depression years, including something called, showers. We thought it might have been a Board of Education-mandated subject from the time when poor children might have taken showers they didn't have at home. We didn't shower during showers; it became an additional gym period.

We were required to take shop—woodworking or sheet metal—and the origin of this subject was likely an intention to teach boys usable vocational skills. In woodworking my group made the traditional Board of Education lamp in the shape of a pump, the pump handle turning the lamp on and off. The shop teacher did not have a future carpenter in me. I labored through shop. He paused along the way in the school year to match our faces to the names in his book. "Who is Corman?" he asked. When I identified myself, he said, "Corman, if you pass shop, my name is Santa Claus." I passed with the help of a couple of my classmates who practically made the entire damn lamp for me.

Typing was a subject we boys dreaded, except for the apples of their enlightened parents' eyes who came into the class already knowing how to type. The keys of the typewriters in the typing room were blacked out. Looking at that menacing keyboard filled us with a feeling close to despair. How would we ever learn on those horrible machines? The woman who taught typing was a perfect complement to the menacing keyboards. She was stern and unremittingly demanding. Taking that class was what it must have been like being in reform school. And, yes, we all learned to touch-type.

The home room teacher of 7SP1 was a disagreeable man. Let's give *him* a break on the name and call him Mr. S____. He carried on a note-passing relationship with a married woman at the school. He may or may not have been married himself. We knew nothing about him. We were to bring his notes to the other teacher and wait to receive notes back. He distributed the messenger assignments among us. On reading her answers to himself in front of us, he would often smile slyly and send a note in return. My last male teacher was the dignified Mr. Katz. Now I had this Mr. S____ enlisting boys with rampant imaginations as the carriers of his messages to an attractive, bosomy woman.

He dropped one of us out of the "SPs." Raymond Nielsen had been my classmate throughout elementary school. A quiet boy and an excellent athlete, he was singled out in 5th grade by Mrs. S____ as part of her ongoing denigration of us. She praised Raymond, declaring him to be "the only he-boy in the class." This gets circumstantial. Mr. S____ was Jewish. Raymond was Protestant. Raymond's father was known to be the superintendent of a building, a super. Was there class bias on Mr. S____'s part? Religious bias? He told us Raymond was no longer in the class, the only one dropped, and Raymond took his place in a conventional 7th grade class, losing the chance to skip a grade.

Academically, the most renowned high school in the Bronx was the Bronx High School of Science. Students were required to take a test for admission to Science and Mr. S____ restricted who could and could not take that test. We decided that he wanted to look good within Board of Education circles with a high percentage of his students getting into the school. He might also have been watching out for us and wanted to shield from disappointment those unlikely to get in or those who would have difficulty at the school if they did get in. This was possibly his motivation, doubtful, but possible. He told me I could not take the test. Was it even within Board of Education regulations for him to prevent me? Since it was prestigious to go there and several of my friends in class were applying and it was one block away from my apartment, I felt badly about it, which was foolish of me. The school stressed science and math where I was weakest and I would have struggled there.

I didn't see much of Raymond after he was transferred out of our class. We had not been close friends and he did not live nearby. A couple of years later when I was in high school I came upon Raymond on the street and we chatted. He had spent his time in the regular Creston classes after being dropped from the "SPs," took the test for the Bronx High School of Science and was accepted. He was a student at Science. So much for Mr. S____'s judgment. Where Raymond Nielsen eventually went after that, what became of him, I am at a loss. I greatly admired him.

I would like to summon the exact details. I cannot remember. I might have talked when I wasn't supposed to. I might have been late to school. I might have thrown Mr. S____ a

disapproving look when he assigned me or one of my classmates the task of delivering one of his precious notes to his
lady friend. Whatever earned his wrath, he announced to the
class that we were going on a trip to the Museum of Natural History and everybody in the class was going except me.
The Creston building was occupied from grades K through 6
by elementary school boys and girls, and 7 through 9 by the
male junior high school students. Mr. S____ told me I was to
spend the day of the trip in a seat in the back of the room in a
1st grade class. He arranged it with a 1st grade teacher who
announced to her little students when I entered the room
that I was there as punishment for bad behavior and I took a
seat that day to the giggling of the little 1st graders.

I asked Richard Kobliner, the person who had told me
about the P.S. 33 reunion, if he knew what became of Mr.
S____. Richard said he had heard he became an assistant
principal or the principal of a school somewhere. Well, good
for you, Mr. S____. You shouldn't have embarrassed a 7th
grader with a punishment like that. You never know who the
7th grader will turn out to be. He just may grow up to be a
writer and write about you.

Those of us who had seen real basketball played in Madison Square Garden and fantasized about playing the game
as it was supposed to be played could act out our fantasies at
Creston in the intramural basketball program. Here was our
first chance to play full court basketball with referees and
foul shots. Our class fielded a competitive team. We had one
of the tallest boys in the grade who went on to play basketball
for Clinton High School and a few other above average players. I was able to be the playmaker just as I had seen it done
in Madison Square Garden.

In junior high school something began, playing organized

basketball, bringing the ball up court, setting up my team-mates, shooting running one-handers. I played basketball in the intramural program at Creston, then the intramural program in high school, on club teams in community centers, on camp counselor teams summers when I worked as a counselor. I wasn't outstanding, not like the players I watched from the sidelines at Creston. For the levels I played at, I was good enough.

I have always felt extraordinarily grateful to my friends from my old neighborhood, those boys I grew up with from the time when we were little kids to when we were teenagers, playing on Creston Avenue and in the the Bronx High School of Science schoolyard. The facts of my family background which seemed so enormous to me didn't matter to them. They didn't care who my father was. They accepted me and that was crucial in my life. First, and most importantly, with my neighborhood friends, and then with organized basketball that began in junior high school, I learned I could be one of the players. I could be like other boys.

THE BRONX ZOO

We could have measured our lives by the Bronx Zoo. When we were little, we were taken to the children's zoo section. We went to the Bronx Zoo by trolley, part of the treat. Trolleys were phased out of the Bronx in the 1940s. Then we were old enough to go with friends rather than with someone from one's family.

The Bronx Zoo was never taken for granted or considered a place meant only for tourists. This was *our* zoo and it was important. On days when the weather was clear and it felt right, my friends and I would say, "This is a zoo day," and we would go. Over the years we explored every part of the place many times over.

The African Plains with its cage-free environment, the animals separated from the public by a moat, was a highlight and a source of conversation among the children of the neighborhood. You think the lions could jump over the moat if they wanted to? What would happen if a lion got out? What would you do? Our imaginations, stimulated by the Johnny

Weissmuller *Tarzan* movies, led us to what-would-happen-if-they-got-out for a variety of the zoo's inhabitants.

The seals, especially at feeding time, were headliners. The duck-billed platypus from Australia was a good novelty and usually attracted lines of visitors—the creature was so odd, a kind of duck and beaver combined.

Before modern zoo environments began to feature simulated natural habitats, the presentation of the inhabitants could be ramshackle, but also could result in appealing exhibits like the penguins close up at ground level in an outdoor enclosure, Charlie Chaplin-ing around.

The first time you went to the zoo with a girl was a big day in your life. The zoo was a logical place to go on a date that wasn't an evening at the movies. It meant you were old enough to be seen walking around with a girl *during the day*.

THE 1951 CITY COLLEGE
BASKETBALL SCANDAL

Our "Say it ain't so, Joe," moment was when the news broke in the winter of 1951 that basketball players from New York City colleges had been rigging the scores of games for gamblers. A national story and a New York City story, for the young people in the neighborhood it was also a Bronx story. Among the City College fixers were three ballplayers who had played for Bronx high schools. Irwin Dambrot and Ed Roman lived in the Bronx and had played for nearby William Howard Taft High School, and Ed Warner had been a star at the Bronx high school many of us attended, DeWitt Clinton.

The news was incomprehensible. As with all local college basketball players, they were major sports figures in New York. These were *our* heroes who had fallen. College basketball was more important than professional basketball. The local college teams played their home games in Madison Square Garden and young sports fans rooted for college teams the way people root for professional teams today. You were an N.Y.U. fan, a City College fan, an L.I.U. fan, and you took sides when they played each other and rooted for the local team when they played a team from elsewhere.

Although the 1951 scandal involved fixers at N.Y.U, L.I.U., Manhattan College, Toledo, Bradley, and Kentucky, in the media it became known as "The City College Basketball Scandal" because of the number of City College players involved and the stature of the City College team.

In the 1949-1950 season, City College won both the NIT and the NCAA championships. The NIT title was more highly regarded than the NCAA then with the games staggered and the finals for both played in Madison Square Garden. With its starting team consisting of former New York City high school ballplayers, City College was the ultimate New York City-style basketball team with considerable ball movement, everybody capable of smoothly handling the ball on offense.

In the NIT tournament, City defeated San Francisco, and then top-ranked Kentucky by 39 points, then Duquesne and Bradley to win the championship. In the NCAA tournament, City defeated Ohio State, North Carolina State, and for a second time in the post-season, Bradley, seven straight unexpected victories in the two tournaments. They were the pride of the city for an instant as a Cinderella Team. Their accomplishment, the double championship, still stands. Teams can no longer play in both tournaments.

The point spread was at the core of the scandal. The players apparently were not trying to lose games. They were trying to win, but by fewer points than the team was favored to win by in the betting line, so the gamblers would collect on their smart bets. The players could walk off the court winners of a game, cheered by their fans, and pocket their payoffs. Less frequently, players were given bonuses for running up the score over the point spread, the gamblers betting those games the other way.

The scandal surfaced when Junius Kellogg of the Manhattan College team reported a bribe offer to his coach. The bribe was brought to the attention of the police and events began to unravel for the fixers and the gamblers. Along with Ed Roman, Irwin Dambrot, and Ed Warner, their City College teammates, Al Roth, Norm Mager, and Floyd Lane were also arrested.

Eventually, we learned City College had rigged the outcomes of games during the very season they ended up winning the double championship. We followed the story, we talked about it—I was fifteen then—we couldn't believe they would do such a thing.

Stanley Cohen, another teenager in the neighborhood, became a writer and as an adult, still absorbed by the scandal, wrote a book about it, *The Game They Played*, named by *Sports Illustrated* as one of the Top 100 Sports Books of All Time.

Thirty-two players were involved, some who were headed for basketball careers in the NBA, including the gifted Sherman White of L.I.U. The new professional league had betting problems of its own. Games were being taken off the board by bookmakers who would not accept bets because they were suspicious of planned outcomes. The NBA was never going to allow players involved in the scandal to play in the league. For the few thousand dollars they each received, the ballplayers were punished dearly. Over the years they did get past the ignominy and put together respectable lives.

The ballplayers caught in the scandal grew up in a city where a distinct betting culture existed in its working class neighborhoods. Many neighborhood people were habituated

horseplayers. Battered by The Depression, people were looking to win bets for the sheer money of it and for whatever
positive feelings they would have from winning. In the Bronx
were the candy stores that attracted bookmakers and bettors. In our neighborhood you could see the more desperate versions of the bettors crouched over their racing forms
day and night in Bickford's Cafeteria, located at the Grand
Concourse and 188th Street near a cars-to-the-track bettors'
candy store. A regular in the candy store and in Bickford's
was the most famous local bookmaker, Joe Hacken, also
known as, Joe Jalop.

When we reached high school, betting cards proliferated
among us, administered by the slicksters in school, the cards
containing the point spreads for the week's upcoming college
football games and we bought the cards and made our picks.

Intrigued by the subject of the fix scandal, when I was
older I went through copies of *The New York Post* and looked
at the point spreads of all the games played in the 1949-
1950 season by the teams that were named to have rigged
points. I compared the point spreads with the final scores
of the games. The New York teams that were said to be fixing games, C.C.N.Y., N.Y.U., L.I.U., and Manhattan College,
failed to win by more than the point spread in far more games
than the District Attorney's office announced as fixed games.
They may not have covered the spread, in gambling parlance,
because that was the way those games played out. But they
may have fixed more games than the District Attorney was
willing to reveal to the public. We will never know. Whether
the fixing of basketball games went beyond the seven colleges
identified is something else we will never know. I suspect the
fixing was more widespread than we were told.

The ballplayers in the scandal had to have been aware of

the extent of gambling in their neighborhoods. They saw the
point spreads listed in the newspapers for every game they
played. They would have heard about NBA games being taken
off the board and the rumors that NBA players were rigging
games, the everybody's-doing-it argument. We can feel sympathy for them if these cultural influences were working on
them and if they felt they were unpaid workers in a business
operation run by their colleges and by Madison Square Garden, with others profiting from their labor. And we can feel
sympathy for them because they paid an extremely high price
for their college-age blunder. But Junius Kellogg reported his
bribe offer. They did this thing and they didn't have to do it.

Shortly after the news of the scandal broke, I was talking
about it with friends in a candy store on 184th Street. One of
the older girls from the neighborhood was listening to us. She
was a student at City College. "For years they've been saying
everyone at City is a Communist," she said, despondent, "and
now this."

EMIL VERBAN

I had an Emil Verban autograph, the only one in the neighborhood, I'm sure. A second baseman with the St. Louis Cardinals, Philadelphia Phillies, and Chicago Cubs from the mid-1940s to 1950, he is known today perhaps only to baseball fanatics. He was a major player to me and I rooted for him.

My mother called me at home from her job at J. W. Mays in Brooklyn and said she helped a baseball player named Emil Verban pick out some children's clothing at the store and he gave her two tickets for the game that night in Ebbets Field against the Dodgers and if I wanted to go I should come out to the store and meet her. We went to the game, Dodgers-Phillies. Coincidentally, one player was signing autographs on the field near the grandstand after the game was over, Emil Verban. I rushed my mother down to where he was standing and he remembered her. They had met only a few hours before. She introduced me, he said hello, shook my hand, and gave me his autograph.

This was neither the first nor the last time my mother took me to a game. When I was growing up she took me to baseball games, football games, basketball games, hockey games. Going to Yankee Stadium or the Polo Grounds was always exciting, but they were nearby. Going downtown to Madison Square Garden was particularly exciting. In her earliest years of working, with very little money at her disposal, selective in what she could manage to do, she would go with me to Sunday afternoon hockey games and we would walk up several flights of stairs to sit in the upper reaches of Madison Square Garden. The tickets for Sunday afternoons didn't cost much, so she could do it—amateur hockey, teams like the Sands Point Tigers, and minor league professional games featuring the New York Rovers, a farm team of the New York Rangers. Sometimes on a special night when there was no school the next day, she spent a little more money and would go up to the balcony with me for a Rangers game.

By the time of high school we could get student discounts to hockey games and I would also go with friends to baseball games. I no longer needed my mother to take me. As she progressed through her business life, she evidenced no interest whatsoever in sports. She never would have gone to a sports event with a friend or watched a game on television. She did ask me to go with her to see plays. She loved theater. The woman she became, successful, well-dressed, sophisticated, to look at her you wouldn't have imagined she once sat high up in the Madison Square Garden balcony for hockey games. Years later, I recalled for her how she took me to games, this in light of her turning out to be completely disinterested in sports. She said, "I thought a boy growing up without a father should go to sports events."

HIGH SCHOOL

The all-around smartest students in the Bronx generally went to the Bronx High School of Science. Administrators at Science and Science graduates have pointed to the school's highly impressive list of distinguished alumni and properly so. But every Bronx high school produced good citizens and people of achievement and some who made a significant impact in the world at large, the likes of Rosalyn S. Yalow, a graduate of Walton High School in the Bronx. After receiving a doctorate in nuclear physics, she worked as a medical researcher at the Bronx Veterans Administration Hospital in the 1940s and went on to be awarded a Nobel Prize in Medicine.

New York City's public high schools predominantly operated on the principle of large schools moving large numbers of students through a large variety of subject offerings. I went to DeWitt Clinton. If I went anywhere else—apart from the Bronx High School of Science, which surely would have been a problem for me—I am positive I would have done as well in the classes in which I did well and I would not have done any better in the classes I stumbled through.

Clinton was located on Mosholu Parkway near the north-ern end of the Grand Concourse. The all-boys school was not a zoned-by-neighborhood high school. About ten percent of the students were African-American, largely from Man-hattan, the rest of the school population mainly came from throughout the Bronx—Jewish, Protestant, and Irish-Amer-ican and Italian-American Catholics who had chosen not to attend Catholic high schools.

In looking over my high school graduation yearbook from the class of 1952, I took note of how many teachers were male. These were most likely the men who entered teaching at the time of The Depression and because they were cultur-ally restricted by their backgrounds they were never candi-dates for jobs in corporate America. Postwar they were well along in their careers and not going anywhere else, as were their female teaching colleagues, restricted by the-smart-girls-become-teachers bias of the time. Several of my high school teachers were markedly superior to the professors I was to have in college.

From the outset at Clinton I started playing basketball in the intramural program and that helped bring the large school down to size. In my home room was my friend, Ben Miller. Ben played guitar and was building up a playlist of folk songs with which to be charming with girls. I considered him highly advanced. We found out if we could get into the school chorus we could be in the home room for the chorus, a home room with few people in it and a relaxed atmosphere. I reasoned I must have been able to sing, since I had been picked out by that music teacher in Hebrew School.

The teacher for chorus, Mrs. Brotman, was quite pleasant in her demeanor and played some notes on the piano and asked me to match the notes with my voice. I could. I was in the chorus. And so was Ben. The home room was informal and there I stayed for the remainder of high school.

The chorus was divided for vocal arrangements into four parts. I was the baritone line above bass and we had first and second tenors. A third of the members of the chorus were African-American. Most of them sang in their church choirs. Because of these students we had a decent chorus.

We sang at assemblies, graduations, and we sang carols in the hallways at Christmas time. I was fairly good at holding my part, but under pressure of performance you could sometimes feel the entire structure collapsing, the bass line and baritone line drifting into the tenor line that was carrying the melody. We would start out singing something like the Fred Waring arrangement of *Dancing in the Dark*, four-part harmony, and by the time we reached the end we were practically singing in unison. Not a bad sound, but not four-part harmony. Sometimes we got it right.

Apart from being in a group with more African-Americans than I ever had contact with before—and more than I would have contact with in college—listening to some of these church choir-disciplined singers and singing along was an uplifting experience. One young man, Gordon Rivers, had a high, soaring tenor voice and was so passionate when he sang, he would completely lose himself in song, never pausing, just singing. Mrs. Brotman would have to call out, "Breathe, Rivers! Breathe!"

The only varsity letter I received in high school was a letter for music, not anything an athletically-minded boy was going to wear on a sweater, still I was happy to have it. As it turned out, being in the chorus was not just gaming the system on home room. Singing with those real singers was wonderful.

When I was finishing my first year of high school, a student protest atypical of those days occurred. All New York City teachers were paid the same salary. Arguing that their specific skills and, in some cases, additional education should be factored into their pay, high school teachers were seeking an increase. Mayor William O'Dwyer, overseeing the New York City budget, refused the high school teachers at a time New York State had just given the teachers' supervisors at the Board of Education a 30% raise in pay.

In protest through the union, the teachers voted to cease participating in extracurricular activities, shutting down high school clubs and sports teams. When I reached school one morning, a crowd was gathered outside, people talking excitedly. Instigated by the teachers, a students' march was planned down the Grand Concourse and we were to meet up with students from Theordore Roosevelt High School and then go on to City Hall. I was in. A march? Playing hooky en masse? Sure, bring back our teams!

At City Hall we became part of a crowd of thousands of shouting students. *The New York Times* reported 10,000 students demonstrated citywide and 3,000 converged on City Hall. The demonstration consisted of students milling about and yelling at the City Hall building and at the police. This was a protest with a limited attention span. I left with the crowd jamming the subway trains leaving the vicinity.

The next day we were back in school amid a troubling rumor. The principal was going to keep a list of everyone who was out of school for the protest and we would be penalized when and if we ever tried to apply for college.

A police department official said the students' demonstration was the work of "subversives." No penalty was exacted against us and no immediate gains were made by the teachers.

The teachers' boycott of extracurricular activities carried through the school year that followed. Under a new mayor, Vincent R. Impellitteri, the teachers were granted an increase, bringing their annual maximum pay to $6,500. We engaged in our one uncommon outburst and settled back into the familiar. Other student demonstrations did not occur. We were in the 1950s and in the Cold War, with public officials looking for Communists in everybody's soup.

While we were in elementary school they had us ducking under our desks on command in classroom drills in case the Russians dropped an A-Bomb on us. Now we were supposed to beware of stealth Commies. Our teachers were required to comply with the Feinberg Act which prohibited New York school teachers from being members of the Communist Party. Even *The New York Times* was not above using the rhetoric of the anti-Communist New York tabloids. A *New York Times* headline was:

FEINBERG ACT BARRING RED TEACHERS UPHELD BY STATE COURT OF APPEALS

"Red Teachers" from *The New York Times*? The witch hunt mood of the day played out in our classrooms at Clinton in that nothing was ever said about the mood of the day. Our teachers were probably fearful of bringing attention to themselves by discussing the nation's preoccupation with Communism and in place of a teaching opportunity we had silence.

My 6th grade teacher had tried to lead a classroom discussion as to whether teachers should be fired if they were members of the Communist Party. I offered that I didn't think anybody should be fired for belonging to anything. After the class a couple of my classmates teased me and the way they did, 6th grade-level teasing, was to call me a Communist.

I became fascinated with the hearings that pitted Senator Joseph McCarthy against Owen Lattimore, an expert on Asia who taught at Johns Hopkins University. I rushed home from school to watch it on television. Lattimore was accused of being a Communist agent by McCarthy. The confrontation was outstanding theater, the feisty Lattimore with brisk, staccato phrasing rebutting the sneering McCarthy: "I am not and never have been a member of the Communist Party." "I hope the Senator will, in fact, lay his machine gun down. He is too reckless, careless, and irresponsible to have a license to use it."

For a high school student, the impact of watching McCarthy in action on television against Lattimore was powerful. Who could be concerned about Communists and Communism after watching Joe McCarthy?

My family was typical of the families I knew in the neighborhood, the only political thing anyone did was vote—for Democrats. We heard of enclaves of Socialists in the east Bronx. The writer, Vivian Gornick, who lived in the east Bronx, has referred in print to her "slightly irreverent left-wing household." Not our household. My mother had cousins with a chicken farm in Tom's River, New Jersey, whom she said were Communists, a notion that seemed to me as far away as a chicken farm in Tom's River, New Jersey.

The patterns that showed up earlier in junior high school became definitive for me in high school, high grades in English and history, low grades in math and science. Combine the numbers and my high school average was 83 at the end.

I was in a history class with some of the better history students. The bell would ring to end the period and they would get up to attend the next class, trigonometry for most of them. I did not join them. I was taking intermediate algebra . . . for . . . the . . . very . . . slow . . . Spread out over two terms instead of one, it was known in school as "Idiot's Algebra."

For my chemistry Regents exam I was sitting in the stairwell outside the classroom still cramming with my Barron's prep book seconds before the exam was to begin.

The principal of the school, Walter Degnan, a strict disciplinarian, enjoyed a grudging admiration among the students — for his foot speed. If he happened to spot anyone leaving the building to cut classes, Mr. Degnan, in his street shoes, would chase after him and usually run him down, a smart tactic in an all-boys school, establishing he was not a man to cross.

A cultural amenity at Clinton were the plays staged by Actors Equity in the school auditorium. Not community theater performed by amateurs, the actors were professionals, members of Actors Equity. The admission price was little more than the cost of a movie ticket and attracted adult Bronx residents and, inasmuch as the performances were staged in our school, Clinton students. I volunteered to be an usher which enabled me to see the plays without paying, productions like *Arsenic and Old Lace, Blithe Spirit, Pygmalion.*

The high school years for people of my age coincided with the Korean War, a gray war at a gray time, a war without bunting. Unlike World War II when our neighborhoods breathed with the events overseas, the public was not galvanized except for those unfortunate to serve and for their families.

From the summer of 1950 to the summer of 1953, the United States tallied more than 35,000 dead, a serious number for what was sometimes called in the media a "police action" and a "conflict," rather than a war. As an elementary school child I had followed the war maps in *The Bronx Home News* during World War II. As a high school student I was now buying *The New York Times* at the candy store downstairs and reading the war coverage on my bus ride to Clinton in the mornings. *The Bronx Home News* was no longer published. Its optimistic slant on war news gone. We received instead in *Life* magazine, David Douglas Duncan's photographs of the faces of American servicemen, portraying how much of a slog was this war.

In 1951, General Douglas MacArthur reinterpreted the chain of command in his own behalf. President Harry S. Truman reasserted civilian control of the military, dismissing McArthur in the middle of the war. MacArthur took a victory lap for his career in a speech before Congress, his "Old soldiers never die" speech. My family voted for Truman as they had for Roosevelt and my allegiance was not with MacArthur. The word, "stalemate," was being used to describe the war, which inched along through the rest of our high school years.

We were proud of our school the way most high school students are proud of their high schools. Our pride did not manifest itself in attending games by our school teams. Most of the people I knew in school did not attend football games. As for the basketball team, when they played a home game sometimes I stayed in school and watched. Less frequently I would attend an away game. With a choice between watching a game played by other people and playing ball ourselves after school, many of us preferred to play ball. My neighborhood friends were mainly distributed between Clinton, Science and several Catholic high schools. They did not customarily attend their school games either. We were still playing schoolyard basketball in the Science and Creston schoolyards as we were growing older, trying to hold on to our relationships with each other.

In the summer before my senior year at Clinton, I was a junior counselor at a sleepaway camp. I returned there as a regular counselor the following summer and worked as a counselor in other camps the next two summers when I was in college. I was fifteen that first summer and went from sitting on the sidelines when others danced at parties, which had been my specialty, to attempted dancing with the girl counselors.

Previous to the summer I had been invited to a party by people I played basketball with on a community center team and I didn't know how to dance well enough to dance. I feigned a foot injury and attended the party limping.

At camp I was so nervous about dancing, I invented my own style of the slow fox trot — very fast. One of my counselor friends called me, "Speedy."

Back in the city I went on a few dates with girls I met through the counselors at camp. Socially, I was about as smooth an operator as I was in math.

A school tradition was for seniors to wear a hat designating them as seniors. Inexplicably, chosen for the senior class hat was a French foreign legion model with a flap hanging from the back. We must have looked absurd to the world at large wearing these hats to school, but we bought them because they announced to everyone at Clinton that we were seniors.

We were coming to the end of high school. Several of my classes had been outstanding and the same could be said by anyone who attended public high schools in the city then with that unusual generation of teachers. I received from a teacher whose name was Dr. Bernhard, a 96 in English, the highest grade I had ever been given. I was very pleased, but that was all. I was unable to see that it might have had some significance.

Clinton had its prized students in the school population, its honor students, its Arista. The main advisor to these boys was "Doc" Guernsey, who had been a pal to the elite students for decades and was beloved by them. My final grade in English did not significantly change my overall academic record. I averaged out to be an average student, so I did not know "Doc" Guernsey, nor did he know me. His colleagues who were friendly with the prized students did not know me either and I did not know them. I passed through high school completely anonymous academically.

THE PARADISE PIZZERIA

The Paradise Pizzeria was our Stork Club. When we started dating this was the place you took a girl you wanted to be seen with because other guys and other girls might be there to see her with you.

Located at 184th Street and Morris Avenue, it was the place people went to after a movie or for a stand-alone meal on an evening out. A legitimate neighborhood restaurant, not a slice joint, The Paradise had size, quite a few tables, and a jukebox. Now and again a neighborhood weisenheimer would drop money in the jukebox on his way out of the place, running away laughing with his friends, leaving behind something like five repeats of an irritating recording like Eddie Fisher's rendition of *Oh! My Pa-Pa.*

Given the number of places there were to buy pizza in the Bronx—which expanded exponentially in the 1950s—and given that the Bronx had its own "Little Italy in the Bronx" area with the Arthur Avenue section of the east Bronx, I would not go near saying The Paradise served the best pizza in the Bronx. I will say it was delicious.

A thought about the Arthur Avenue area. For my sister, cousins, and their boyfriends, Arthur Avenue was an eating destination—sometimes they brought me along—the Arthur Avenue area featuring the first steak house many Bronx residents ever went to, Dominick's, eventually superseded by another Dominick's. The original Dominick's was pridefully regarded by Bronxites as good as any steak restaurant downtown. I wouldn't have been able to weigh in on that, never having eaten in a steakhouse downtown.

To the rear of the Concourse Center of Israel synagogue was a small chapel on Creston Avenue, wood-shingled with a few outside stairs, the small house used for daily prayer service. Those stairs became a neighborhood hangout for the boys and girls from the immediate vicinity. We took turns sitting on the steps, at times only the boys while the girls leaned against cars or gathered nearby, at times, the reverse. And at times we mixed, with the spillover extending to the sidewalk. Testing out our emerging mental capacities, we would play charades together and sometimes order pizza from the Paradise.

The pizza at the Paradise Pizzeria was the first pizza I knew and I carry the Paradise pizza memory with me. The pizza had a distinct tomato sauce taste. The cheese, which was not excessive, and the tomato sauce were in balance, not like those pies, soggy with cheese, the taste of tomato sauce indiscernible, that now pass for "New York pizza." To this day when I eat pizza I look for that element of tomato sauce. Six decades later I'm still comparing pizza with the pizza at The Paradise Pizzeria.

GETTING TO ARTHUR AVENUE

A few years ago, I was on the platform of the 86th Street and Lexington Avenue subway station and I noticed four people, obviously tourists, looking at a map. I asked if I could help. One of them said, "We're trying to get to Arthur Avenue in the Bronx." "Okay," I responded. "Go downstairs and take the Number Four to the Bronx and get off at Fordham Road. When you get off, transfer to a bus going east toward the Bronx Zoo. Ask somebody. Make sure you're going toward the zoo. Tell the driver you want Arthur Avenue and can he call out the stop. When you get off the bus, walk in exactly the direction you're facing, which will be south. A few blocks and you'll find the area you're looking for. If the driver forgets and you reach the zoo, you've gone a couple of blocks too far." "Thanks," one of them said, very offhandedly, and they blithely went along their way. I had to smile. They probably thought—ask any New Yorker for directions and he'll tell you how to go. In a ten-block radius there was probably nobody other than me, including the subway clerk, who could have given them those exact, correct directions.

CHINESE RESTAURANTS

Wherever you went, whatever the neighborhood in the Bronx, the food in Chinese restaurants was exactly the same. The cooking was indistinguishable from one Chinese restaurant to the next, the same gelatinous dishes, the same "one from column A, one from column B" dinners, the same combination plates—chicken chow mein, egg roll, and fried rice, the same egg drop soup. Chinese restaurants were so much the same, it was as though every one of the places was part of a huge chain.

People have tried to explain the appeal of Chinese restaurants in working class neighborhoods, specifically, among Jewish families. I'm not sure the explanations can go very deep. These were inexpensive meals and for people without much money, Chinese restaurants allowed them to dine out. In our family, and from what I could observe from the dining habits of friends' families, eating Chinese food meant eating *in* the restaurants. We didn't order take-out to eat at home. We didn't eat Chinese food to eat Chinese food. Eating in a restaurant, being served by a waiter, was the idea, and at those prices it was possible.

Chinese restaurants were commonplace; we had three within a few blocks of our apartment. How Sunday night came to be the main night of the week for Chinese food—I don't think the explanation for that goes very deep either. Sunday was considered a family day, so for a Sunday family dinner in a restaurant people could afford, Sunday meant Chinese food.

When we reached dating age, we would sometimes take a girl for a Chinese meal after a movie and so we ate in Chinese restaurants other than those closest to our apartments. The food was still always the same. Whether the food in Bronx Chinese restaurants was ever good by any kind of culinary standards—we didn't have culinary standards. We knew what we were eating was what we had before, what it always was wherever we went, whether the place had "Jade" or "Joy" or "Garden" in the name. It was Chinese.

THE CONCOURSE PLAZA HOTEL

Standing royally at the intersection of 161st Street and the Grand Concourse, located near some of the most elegant apartment buildings on the Grand Concourse, the Concourse Plaza Hotel was the most famous Bronx landmark that had absolutely nothing to do with us in the neighborhood.

With apartment suites for the well-to-do, as a hotel for some of the ballplayers playing at Yankee Stadium, a venue for luncheons and meetings by civic groups that were reported in *The Bronx Home News,* where Bronx Democratic bosses, Edward J. Flynn and then Charles A. Buckley brought campaigning Democrats to political luncheons, Franklin D. Roosevelt and Harry S. Truman among them, where people were married and where bar mitzvah receptions were held in its ballrooms. The Concourse Plaza, several subway stops to the south, was in a different economic sphere, a building we had no reason to ever be in. Nearby to the Concourse Plaza was another Bronx landmark, the Bronx County Courthouse, also a building we had no reason to ever be in.

I was in the Concourse Plaza Hotel only once in my years

of living in the Bronx. I was brought to a sweet sixteen party by a girl I was dating, the birthday girl a schoolmate of hers. The birthday girl lived in 1150 Grand Concourse, an art deco elevator building famous for its aquatic mosaic on the facade, decidedly a "better" building in the Bronx, so that was consistent with the girl having her sweet sixteen party at the Concourse Plaza.

The sweet sixteen event was part of a string of sweet sixteen parties of girls I knew, or by way of boys who knew the girls. Needing to bring something as gifts, with little sense of what you should bring a girl for a gift, I brought them umbrellas. Nice umbrellas, but umbrellas.

JACK MOLINAS

I knew Jack Molinas, as we used to say, by face. If we would pass on the street, I would nod, he would nod. I was four years younger than Jack, vast in the neighborhood hierarchy. It wasn't age alone that accounted for the distance between us. At his eventual height, 6 feet 6, he walked through the neighborhood streets with striking self-awareness. Jack Molinas was a star.

And then—it's baffling. Four books have been written about him, three of them novels as if the bewildering nature of his story can't be properly expressed in other than fictional terms—*Big Time* by Phil Berger (1990), *The Great Molinas* by Neil D. Isaacs (1992), *Broken Trust* by Jerry Marcus (2008), and a biography, *The Wizard of Odds* by Charley Rosen (2001).

In his biography, Charley Rosen quotes Hubie Brown, the television analyst and as an NBA coach a member of the Basketball Hall of Fame. "Jack Molinas was one of the greatest players to play the game of basketball. Molinas was a perfect player and by that I mean he wasn't a specialist. He could handle and pass, play defense if he wanted to, and rebound in a crowd if he wanted to. He had a great assortment of head fakes and ball fakes. He was a savvy player with great timing, and his extra edge was his phenomenal hook shot, the best hook shot ever. There was nothing Jack Molinas couldn't do on a basketball court."

Jack Molinas was murdered in 1975, shot to death by a hit man in Los Angeles. At the time of his death Jack was to stand trial on charges of shipping pornographic films from Los Angeles to Memphis. Nicholas Gage wrote in *The New York Times*, "Law enforcement officials say Mr. Molinas was involved with Mafia members in the distribution and production of pornographic films both in Los Angeles and New York."

Frank Lombardi reported in *The Daily News* that in 1977 the LAPD made arrests for Jack's murder. A man named Eugene Connor was identified as the hit man. Two accomplices of Connor told the Los Angeles District Attorney's office, Lombardi reported, that the hit was ordered by Joseph Ullo, a crime figure who had come to Los Angeles from New York. The men claimed Jack had an outstanding gambling debt and Ullo was looking to collect and capture part of the money and ordered the hit when Jack refused to pay.

The trial for Jack's murder was held in 1979. The two accomplices testified against Connor and Ullo. There was insufficient evidence to link Ullo to the crime and he was acquitted. Connor was found guilty and sentenced to life for the murder.

Over time a theory was advanced that Ullo did order the hit, but was not acting out of personal grievance, rather he was directed by a higher level of the mob to see that Jack was killed. Whoever it was who actually ordered Jack's murder, that person was never convicted.

I just happened to be in an apartment of a school friend who knew Jack and had invited him to stop by on the same night the news came over the radio about the 1950-51 college point shaving scandal. On hearing the news report, Jack left abruptly saying, "I know some of those people."

If anyone was caught up in the culture of gambling in the neighborhood it was Jack Molinas. He was a regular at the cars-to-the-track candy store near Bickford's Cafeteria, and the bookmaker, Joe Hacken, was often seen openly talking to Jack in the store. Joe Hacken even sponsored a basketball team and Jack and several of the best ballplayers from the area played on the team, The Hacken All-Stars. A bookmaker organizing a basketball team? And naming it after himself? Interesting times.

That Jack Molinas was friendly with a bookmaker, that he knew "some of those people" who were involved in a betting scandal, and that he favored a candy store where bettors used to hang out was foreshadowing, which in a play or movie would have been obvious foreshadowing at that.

Jack's first basketball success came when he was playing for Stuyvesant High School and from there he went to Columbia University. As captain and high scorer of the team, he led Columbia to the Ivy League championship in the 1952-53 season. He was a first round draft pick in the NBA of the Fort Wayne Pistons and in his rookie season, the 1953-54 season, he was named to the All-Star team. Jack never played in the All-Star game. He was found to be betting on Pistons games, which was against league policy, and was suspended by the NBA commissioner, Maurice Podoloff.

The talk in the neighborhood was that the NBA was riddled with tainted games. Podoloff might have been looking to use Jack to deflect criticism and in the process send a message to the players. Or he might have legitimately felt this was what the situation called for. The suspension was punitive. It became a permanent suspension. In a similar situation ten years later, Paul Hornung of the Green Bay Packers and Alex Karras of the Detroit Lions were suspended for betting on NFL games. They were reinstated after one year.

Jack turned around, went to law school, graduating from Brooklyn Law School in 1959, joined a law firm, and prepared a suit against the NBA for reinstatement and damages. He was playing in the Eastern League, a minor league with ballplayers a cut below NBA level, along with some NBA-level players who were also barred from the NBA, having been involved in the 1950-51 scandal. Jack was a dominant player in the league.

I can't possibly understand what happened next, not that I could understand why Jack would throw his professional basketball career into jeopardy in order to make side bets. *While* working as a lawyer, *while* playing in the Eastern League to stay in condition for a possible reinstatement by the NBA, *while* he had legal action pending against the league, *while* he had knowledge of how the 1950-51 point shaving enterprise ended—the main gambler-fixer, Salvatore Sollazzo, was caught and imprisoned—Jack enlisted some pals and organized a large, complex ring of his own for bribing college basketball players to fix the scores of college games and profit from tactical betting on those games.

Along the way, in 1961, he lost his lawsuit against the NBA. Judge Irving R. Kaufman, the judge who sentenced the Rosenbergs to death, ruled against him.

In Jack's operation his main people were friends of his, Joe Green, Aaron Wagman, and Joe Hacken. All eventually went to jail when the scheme unraveled. He had enlisted at least six other people who were also indicted. It was reported in *The New York Post* by Phil Berger and Stu Black that Jack was in business on the money side with "mob-backed gamblers."

Jack's betting ring involved forty-nine basketball players in twenty-five colleges in eighteen states. That really needs to be restated, forty-nine players, twenty-five colleges, eighteen states. How could he ever think he would get away with something so large and complicated? And why would he ever do it in the first place?

Because of Jack's scheme the college ballplayers who were implicated had their lives turned upside down and his friends ended up in prison. Joe Hacken, an experienced bookmaker, had to know the risks he was taking by trying to rig scores, and on such a large scale. Joe Green was someone I used to see around the neighborhood. I had no idea what he did for a living. He was a rough looking, linebacker-type guy, but I always thought him to be a benign character and had no evidence to the contrary. Aaron Wagman, whom I knew, was just another neighborhood guy, also benign.

When the betting operation was exposed, Aaron Wagman chose to become a witness for the prosecution. *The New York Times* reported he received "a suspended sentence conditioned on his serving a five-to-10 year sentence in Florida for fixing a football game," Aaron having gone off on a scheme of his own. Joe Green was sentenced to six to seven years. Joe Hacken was sentenced to seven and a half to eight years. Of the six other people in the "Molinas Ring," as *The New York Times* identified the group, five received suspended sentences, the sixth was sentenced to jail.

In his book, Charley Rosen suggests the kind of arrogance and denial Jack must have been operating under. "Before the trial began," he writes, "Molinas was offered a deal—admit that he'd masterminded several fixes in exchange for having his license to practice law revoked and serving a six months' sentence. Molinas refused."

He was found guilty. The sentence was ten to fifteen years, so harsh it was eventually reduced on appeal to a still significant seven to eleven and a half years, and Jack Molinas of Stuyvesant High School, captain of the Ivy League Championship Columbia basketball team, chosen an NBA All-Star in his rookie year, a Brooklyn Law School graduate, and a practicing lawyer, was sent to Attica prison.

At Attica he attempted to have his time reduced by offering to the Brooklyn District Attorney's office information about a harness racing fix scheme he knew about possibly through his commerce with the "mob-backed gamblers" *The New York Post* mentioned. He also offered information about a check swindle operation. His cooperation on the harness racing scheme was reported in *The New York Times*, so he was publicly identified as an informant, a risk he was willing to take, and his sentence was indeed reduced, Jack leaving Attica after four years.

He was able to get his parole jurisdiction switched from New York to Los Angeles, ostensibly so he could sell his life story to the movies. A movie was not made.

In Los Angeles, he became partners with Bernard Gusoff in a wholesale fur business. They took out life insurance policies on each other and only weeks before the policies were to expire, Gusoff was murdered, beaten to death. Jack collected $500,000 on Gusoff's life insurance. No one was ever convicted for the murder.

Arnie Stein, someone else I also knew in the neighborhood by face, played basketball for Taft High School and then for

Dayton University. He was a friend of Jack. I recognized him in a restaurant he owned in Manhattan. One evening we talked about Jack. "His father was very strict, abusive, really," Arnie said, "and I think Jack lived a life to get back at his father, to humiliate him." Later in the conversation, he said, "I always thought Jack was somebody who was trying to find a way of committing suicide."

Arnie Stein, Bobby Santini, another friend of Jack, who starred at Iona College, and Dolph Schayes, a few years older than Jack, were major basketball players from the neighborhood. They were of the same neighborhood background at the same time, a time when betting on horse racing, boxing, and ball games among the working class men of the neighborhood was common. They were subject to the same cultural pressures and influences. Arnie Stein became a businessman and restaurateur, Bobby Santini, a teacher, Dolph Schayes was named one of the 50 Greatest Players in NBA history. And Jack became Jack.

Charley Rosen in his biography writes, "In the final analysis, however, it appears that Jack's misdeeds were fueled by that most ancient and universal of sins, hubris. He was too smart. Too smart to think the rules applied to him. Too smart to imagine he could ever get caught."

Because the trajectory of Jack Molinas's life is so bewildering, we have had those four books written about him. The narrative line of his story has the capacity to make one feel superior. This was a person of uncommon abilities, he spiraled into the dark and tawdry, meanwhile look at what *I* accomplished, one could say, and that would fit nearly anyone, any accomplishment, since the comparison is with someone who self-destructed and became a disbarred lawyer, a convicted felon, and was murdered. It is for me, though, one of the most upsetting stories of the old neighborhood. Jack Molinas, purely the basketball star, before all his wheeling and dealing, when he walked through the neighborhood with his self-confident stride, owned those streets. As a young man he was so luminous that when he passed me on the sidewalk and nodded, nodded acknowledging me, I felt good about myself.

LAUREL & HARDY GO ICE SKATING

Under a Carolina moon, my friend, Freddy Krongold, told a French-Canadian girl from a small town in Canada that he was an expert ice skater. Freddy had never ice skated. After high school he studied to be a draftsman and was working as a draftsman in jobs around the country. On one of these road jobs he met the girl who was herself traveling and working. He thought it was safe in a balmy Southern locale to endear himself to her by bragging about his skating prowess. Unfortunately, he had fallen for her and was to travel to a Canadian town with a French name he couldn't pronounce properly to meet her family. Her brothers were going to be very pleased to meet him, she told Freddy, and were looking forward to going ice skating with him.

Freddy lived in my building and home for a visit, he came to me, beleaguered. He was standing in the doorway of my apartment holding hockey-style ice skates he had just purchased. He needed me to go ice skating with him. He had to learn in a hurry. He had about an hour to spare for it and then he was traveling to see her in Canada. We had known each other for years, I would have done anything for Freddy, but I needed to point out to him that he was asking the wrong guy. I didn't know how to ice skate either. He didn't care. He had to learn this and in a hurry. I suggested he was never going to learn well enough to pull it off. He insisted we try, that I go with him and somehow it would work out.

We had a neighborhood ice skating rink. We didn't grow up with it or we might have known how to ice skate. The arrival of television claimed one Bronx movie house after another, and in an attempt to salvage the space, the Oxford Theater, a few blocks away, had been converted to an ice rink. I went there with Freddy and rented skates. He wore his newly purchased pair. This was a low-rent rink, the walls were movie theater walls. Only a couple of people were on the ice, no skating instructor was available, not even a rink attendant, and locking arms, we slid onto the ice, our feet flew out from under us and we landed resoundingly on our derrières. For about an hour we skidded all over the rink, constantly falling, crashing into the side walls. Our best move was to grab onto each other for support and fall to the ice together.

We might have been making a little progress, I mean, a little, but the progress was not on the level of Freddy being able to get out on the ice and skate with boys from a Canadian town with a French name he couldn't pronounce properly. We were falling less frequently, but still falling, like snow.

Bruised, aching, we left. Freddy said he would think of something, but skating wasn't it.

I should note that somewhere in Freddy's courting of this girl he suggested to her that he might convert to Catholicism. He told me he went to church with her and the priest was very impressed with how pious he looked. Freddy said the priest was mistaken about his pious look. Freddy, another

Jewish boy who never went to services, admitted to me he was merely bored.

A couple of weeks later, Freddy came to my door and presented me with his ice skates. They were mine. He was never going to put them on again. He made up a story in Canada that he wasn't feeling well and got out of going ice skating with the brothers. He saw the girl for a while. The relationship didn't last. Eventually, he married someone else.

I went back to the rink and figured enough out so that I could get around and stop myself by grabbing on to the side board. I used the skates when I moved to Manhattan because taking a girl to Wollman Rink in Central Park was a pretty nifty cheap date. Some of the girls didn't know how to skate and I encouraged them to try, saying I would show them. Nothing to it. I had Freddy's skates a long time and then the leather gave out. I wore them skating with my children.

ABSENCE OF A MANILA ENVELOPE

He was the only man in the neighborhood I ever saw carrying a manila envelope. And nobody carried a briefcase. I later learned the man, my friend's father, worked in photoengraving and took proofs home at night to check them. The absence of a manila envelope or a briefcase in the possession of the men going to and from work each day helped define my old neighborhood as working class.

My friend's father held an office job. Most of the men did not. The majority of the women stayed at home, my mother in the minority. Doctors, lawyers, businessmen were known to live in the Bronx—most likely in the art deco elevator buildings on the Grand Concourse, in the Pelham Parkway area, in the prestigious Lewis Morris Apartments on the Grand Concourse near 174th Street, or in the more affluent Riverdale section of the Bronx.

Geographically, Riverdale was located in the Bronx, but we never considered Riverdale in the northwest part of the borough, with its new apartment buildings and many private homes, as *really* the Bronx and Riverdale residents welcomed

that distinction. People didn't say they came from the Bronx
if they came from Riverdale.

A few elevator buildings and private homes were located in
our neighborhood and the adjacent neighborhoods. Largely
it was building after building, block after block of similar
undistinguished-looking walk-up apartment houses inhabited by working class residents.

At 1940s and 1950s prices and apartment rents, a Bronx
man could earn no more than $100 a week in the pay scale
of those years and raise a family. And with the free tuition
City University system in place then, his children could go
to college. Within the earnings limitations of the trades the
men worked in or the stores they owned, many of them must
have thought they were doing well for living in the Bronx.
The Bronx was still a step up from the lower east side and the
tenement sections of Manhattan where many of their parents
and perhaps they themselves had lived.

If the urban blight in the Bronx which began in the 1960s
had never occurred, the demographics of the Bronx still
would have changed from the years when I grew up there.
Take this one person as an example. Martin Garbus attended
Bronx neighborhood public schools and then the Bronx High
School of Science. He was among the first male students to
graduate from tuition-free Hunter College in the Bronx and
then went to N.Y.U. Law School. Martin Garbus became a
prominent attorney and author. His father owned a candy
store in the Bronx. The educated children of Bronx working
class parents, children who grew up in the 1940s and 1950s,
people like Martin Garbus, were not going to remain in the
Bronx. They were going to leave for a different way of life
from their parents, so they could one day carry the manila
envelopes and the briefcases their parents did not.

THE TAN JACKET

Going with my mother to buy my clothes was extremely awkward. I would look around to see if anybody was watching. It was important to reach the point when I could go on my own to buy things for myself and that was about the time I was high school age.

When I was in college and needed a sports jacket, I went by myself to the Simon Ackerman store near Fordham Road and picked out a sports jacket I thought was really nice looking and fit well, a tan jacket with a lighter tan thread through it, a near-plaid effect. I was very pleased with my jacket until I wore it in the presence of someone who went to the University of Pennsylvania, a friend of a college classmate of mine. My classmate's friend made a remark about the jacket, that it was okay, but nothing *he* would ever wear. He preferred darker colors for his clothing, which he bought at Brooks Brothers.

I needed to wear the jacket, but from then on I felt ill at ease about it, that a guy from Penn wouldn't wear it, that my choice of this jacket made a statement about me, about social class.

I found a picture of myself recently and I was wearing the jacket I had come to feel so ill at ease about. It was a very nice jacket and I looked terrific in it.

COLLEGE

In our neighborhood most of us who were college-bound were headed for colleges in New York City. City College, Hunter College, N.Y.U., Fordham, Columbia were the main New York City colleges attended by people I knew.

One boy from the neighborhood said his parents, postal workers, created a savings fund when he was born and he was able to go to an out-of-town college. Sounded brilliant to me. He chose Ohio State. Bobby Santini, the basketball player, went to Iona College in New Rochelle, close to New York City. His older brother, Billy, went to Notre Dame. That was the extent of the people I knew of who lived nearby going to colleges that were not in the city. So few of us went to out-of-town colleges simply because our families couldn't afford it.

People like my friend, Ben Miller, who were good in math, were planning on going to schools of engineering, in his case, City College. In the Cold War 1950s, it was nearly patriotic to study engineering. America needed engineers to compete with the Russians, it was said, and the jobs were there. *The New York Times* ran pages of want ads for engineers.

Leslie Zucker, one of my classmates at Creston who went to the Bronx High School of Science, knew that he was going to be a dentist. I didn't know anything. I had skipped that term in junior high and merely by completing a certain number of classes, skipped another term at Clinton, so I was a high school senior making my college decision as I turned sixteen, as did others in my situation. But in my case, my ignorance about myself cannot be understated. This was my reasoning: I wasn't good at math, so I couldn't study engineering. I wasn't good at science, so I couldn't study medicine. I didn't like memorizing, so I couldn't go to law school. Business remained. I would go into business. My mother worked in business, my cousin was in business. He had moved from motion picture publicity to selling movies to television stations. Business, an amorphous thought, business, was the place for me, I concluded. I ignored that my scores had been high in English and history and never considered being a liberal arts major somewhere. I thought my smart choice was to apply to a business college. In a family discussion with my mother and sister, I offered my intelligent analysis of myself, why I should go to a school for business.

I assumed my mother could have afforded to send me to an out-of-town college, but when I expressed my preference to go out of town, my sister, who was then married, uncharacteristically did not support me. She said, "How can you go to college out of town and leave Mother alone?" I wasn't going to endorse the idea of being company for my mother forever. At age sixteen, I complied and looked into the main undergraduate business schools in New York City. They were City College downtown on 23rd Street and N.Y.U. on Washington Square. Whether it was merited or not, the business college at N.Y.U. seemed to be slightly more prestigious than City

College, if for no other reason than you paid to attend. My mother offered that she could afford it and the consensus was my first choice should be N.Y.U. and I was accepted there.

In the 1950s, the N.Y.U. School of Commerce, Accounts, and Finance was essentially a trade school which granted a diploma to be used for finding work. Students were required to take half their courses in liberal arts and half in business subjects. Both sides of the curriculum were lackluster. The liberal arts courses were an academic notch below the English and history courses of my senior year of high school. The business courses included invented subjects, such as a course in which you watched movies, industrial films created to promote industries, like the latest developments in the canning industry.

Traveling to school by subway each day was like going to a job. My classes were completed in the early afternoon and I worked part-time after classes in the stacks of the 42nd Street Library.

A requirement for graduation was a semester each of bookkeeping and accounting during freshman year. Another version of math to me, I managed to pass with my nose barely over the finish line.

The social character of the school was partly influenced by the presence of the students enrolled in the School of Retailing within the college. These students, primarily female, were looking forward to jobs as retail store buyers and executives. The female students came to school dressed for the future, usually wearing high heels and clothing similar to the kind my mother wore to work—a school where the girls dressed like your mother.

None of them were ever going to go out with me. I was too young for them and the way I dressed compared to the way they dressed, I was probably too gauche. I wore a sweater and jeans. In cooler weather, a raincoat. In my first years of college, I was still dating high school girls, hoping, as they turned up, that they were at least high school seniors.

We boys in the neighborhood, in dreamland, bought condoms from our friendly pharmacist. We kept a condom in our wallet, just in case. It left a ring on your wallet, which was inclined to happen when you never had reason to remove it.

The girls I dated during my college years came largely by way of blind dates—through fellow counselors at the children's camps where I worked, through new friends I made at N.Y.U., through girls I didn't connect with, but who were willing to pass me along to someone else. One of the counselors, an older fellow who was in graduate school, told me, "You know, when you go out with a girl, she's just as nervous as you." This was helpful. I didn't really know that.

Of all those dates, all those girls, somehow I remember one evening in particular. Who arranged the blind date, I do not remember. My date lived in an apartment building in the east Bronx and perhaps nothing suitable was playing in the movies, or it was suggested by the go-between, and we ended up not going out, just sitting in her living room talking so as to get to know each other. She was a plain girl, extremely shy, extremely quiet. I knew the requisite chemistry was lacking and I wasn't going to see her again, but I was appropriate. I stayed a couple of hours, talking, and then I said it was time to leave, except she said something that held me in place. "But I bought a cake." She had gone to the bakery and bought a cake for her blind date, a cake that was in a box on the kitchen table. I said that was nice and we should have some and she cut a slice of cake for each of us, and we sat at her kitchen table and talked some more and ate the cake, and

I thanked her for it and left knowing I was not going to call her again, not knowing these many years later I would recall an extremely shy, extremely quiet girl who bought a cake.

An advantage of going to school downtown was that you became familiar with different places to go on dates, which was important since you were always trying to show what a sharp guy you were—performances of Brother Theodore and his tales from Ambrose Bierce and Edgar Allan Poe. Greenwich Village coffee houses. An Italian restaurant near N.Y.U. where men played bocce while you ate. Broadway shows—in the second balcony. Greenwich Village art movie houses. Staying in the Bronx would work, too, if you took a girl to the Ascot, still showing foreign films.

Ben Miller and his folk singing widened his base of operations and he included me. He met some private school girls, high school seniors, and I went out with one of them. I mentioned to a friend that where the girl lived, in a duplex apartment on Central Park West overlooking the park, was the most beautiful apartment I had ever been in. My friend, who was from the Bronx, began referring to her as, "Duplex Annie," thinking he was being clever, unaware he was responding with hostility to the difference in backgrounds.

My dating relationship with the girl lasted only a few dates. I remained friendly with her for a while afterward. She went on to Sarah Lawrence College and fixed me up with a couple of her college friends. Sarah Lawrence in Bronxville was not far from where we lived and a neighborhood friend of mine with a car went on a double date with me. We took our Sarah Lawrence dates to a restaurant in the Bronx near Long Island Sound. Considering how much we were prepared to spend for a first date, and a blind date at that, we thought it was a pretty good place—with a dance floor, the music supplied by a juke box. The girls' attitude indicated it was not to their standards. "Guess you're not going all out," one of them said sardonically. Another time a girl from Sarah Lawrence stayed at the Central Park West apartment so I could go out with her. Somehow the subject of dogs came up. She owned nine dogs, she said. I asked what you would do with nine dogs. "We hunt," she answered.

These were girls who went away to spend college weekends with Ivy League boys. My brief period of dating these girls as a boy from the Bronx was heavy with implications about stations in life and uncomfortable.

My mother wanted to live in a place more suitable to her improved economic status. She chose an area of the Grand Concourse where elevator buildings predominated and stores did not occupy the street level. 1695 Grand Concourse was an elevator building just south of the Lewis Morris Apartments near 174th Street. The kitchen and bathroom fixtures in the new apartment were modern, the tree-lined Grand Concourse, without stores, was picturesque here. The Bronx is what my mother knew, where she wanted to be and it is indicative of her feelings about the place and the stability of the Bronx in the 1950s that she could think of a move from one part of the Bronx to another as upwardly mobile.

The time when our neighborhood friends were our friends exclusively had been changing as we went to our different colleges. We seldom had time to spare for schoolyard basketball. Because I worked part-time, I hadn't been socializing in the neighborhood as I once did, and as I proceeded at N.Y.U. even the banal course work required study and term papers. Others had demands on their time. Our growing-up neighborhood life was ending. And it was ending at the very time I moved away from the neighborhood.

After my latest summer as a camp counselor I returned with what I considered to be a new intelligent self-assessment. As a camp counselor, I wrote lyrics for parodies of pop songs for Color War and other camp events and discovered I had a flair for it. I had chosen the business world. I was in a business college and if I had a way with words I decided what I would do with it. I would become an advertising copywriter.

I began to major in marketing and started taking courses in advertising. One of my classmates, Marty Daniels, worked on the business side of the college newspaper and suggested I join him on the staff. I worked on the newspaper selling advertising space to Greenwich Village stores and restaurants and I wrote ads for the advertisers. When N.Y.U. combined the newspapers for the three undergraduate colleges on Washington Square into one newspaper, I became the business manager. The newspaper office was a hangout for people who worked on the paper, for their friends, for students trying to get articles into print about some area of their interest. The place was alive, a contrast to my moribund classes. I no longer worked part-time after school. I was in the newspaper office every day.

One of the people who wrote for the paper was Elliot Denman, a premier race walker who competed for N.Y.U. and went on to represent the United States in the 1956 Olympics. He thought it would be fun for me to try out for the N.Y.U. track team as a walker and he also approached a classmate of ours. An event was coming up in Madison Square Garden, the intercollegiate indoor track and field championships. A one-mile walk was scheduled. With that event in mind, Elliot showed us the proper race walking techniques and we practiced with him, using as a track, the sidewalk encircling Yankee Stadium. He then took us to the Bronx N.Y.U. campus where the track team practiced on an outdoor track under the coach, Emil von Elling. As we went around the track doing the heel-and-toe stride Elliot taught us, he spoke to the coach. We were placed on the track team. We practiced for a couple of weeks for the event at Madison Square Garden, which was held on a Saturday afternoon. *The* Madison Square Garden and I was in it, wearing a competitor's number at a track meet with a public address announcer calling off events and with people in the stands.

In practices, the other newcomer was faster than I was for short bursts. I was able to outdistance him over the length of a mile. When the race began his strategy was to block me from getting ahead of him. We became involved in a heated duel jockeying for position, preposterously far behind everyone else in the race. My adversary was disqualified for running, was ordered off the track and with a clear path I finished dead last. Elliot won. I was so dead last they were taking up the boards at one end to make way for the upcoming 60-yard dash when someone yelled, "Hold it, there's someone still on the track."

Some of our friends came to watch and afterward one of them said, "We were laughing so hard, we almost fell out of the balcony."

Another event was scheduled at the armory on 142nd Street and Fifth Avenue as part of the indoor season and it included a one-mile walk handicap race where you were given a head start based on your previous performances in competition. My fellow newcomer did not enter. I did and received a 300-yard handicap, the maximum. Twelve walkers competed. Two of the others lined up at my starting position with the maximum handicap. The competition was held with some ceremony, a band played as you went around the quarter-mile track.

I lost control of my pace which was supposed to be based on my practice times of the past month. I went too fast and—in a one-mile walk race—nearly collapsed from exhaustion as I crossed the finish line. They had to help me off the track. I didn't finish last. Somehow I managed to finish ahead of one of the two who started with me and another who couldn't make up my considerable head start. I was tenth out of twelve. With that accomplishment, I retired from the track team, sports news which went unreported.

With my college years coming to an end, I was convinced I had outstanding credentials. I would be a graduate of a business college. I had specialized in advertising courses and had been the business manager of my college newspaper. I wrote ads that appeared in the newspaper and also had samples of ads from my advertising copy courses, which I was able to assemble in a portfolio. How many people graduating from college competing with me for jobs would have accomplished that much, I said to myself. I heard that sometimes in an advertising agency you needed to take a job in the mailroom and spend a certain amount of time there as part of your apprenticeship toward becoming a copywriter and that was all right with me.

None of the parents of my Bronx friends were college graduates. We were the first and the expectation was for us to accomplish something with our college degrees. In my case, I had an additional incentive, to not be my father's son. I was not going to be anything like him. I was going to do something I never heard of anyone in my old neighborhood doing, none of the older men, none of the younger men. I was going to be an advertising agency copywriter on Madison Avenue.

THE REALITY

It never happened. Prior to my graduation, I sent my resume to advertising agencies, registered with employment agencies and with the college job placement office and covered the classified ads. I did not hear from anyone. I was aware of the difference in the advertising business between advertising agencies that primarily handled consumer accounts and agencies that primarily handled industrial accounts. The prestige was with the agencies with consumer accounts. As my graduation passed and the weeks went by without an interview, I would have been willing to work in any kind of advertising agency.

When four months passed since my first inquiries, I thought about going into the Army and being done with it. The draft was still in effect. Every male had to factor it in. College graduates were being hired, though. Not every employer was demanding that a candidate for a job had to have his military service out of the way. And I was only twenty. From what I had heard, I had a few years before the draft would get to me. I decided to press on.

In my gloomiest moments in the time that followed, I tallied my miscalculations. I should have had the Army out of the way; I made a mistake by not removing that obstacle. I should have tried even harder, been more imaginative in my approach. Above all else, I should not have taken the job I eventually accepted. It was not with an advertising agency, nor was my second job, and each year that passed without working in an advertising agency, I fell behind the graduates who *were* hired by advertising agencies, who did their apprenticeships in mailrooms and in junior copywriter programs, who were already copywriters, and it became too late for me. I was too far along the way in the wrong direction.

By accepting culpability for my unfulfilled hopes, I did not consider the entire equation. Being Jewish with a Bronx address on my resume, graduating from "NY Jew," as the school was sometimes snidely called, and breaking into the Madison Avenue advertising world of the mid-1950s, where many of the people hired for entry level jobs went to the very schools the Sarah Lawrence girls visited on college weekends, didn't seem like an insurmountable obstacle to me. As I neared graduation I had heard at school that Grey Advertising and Doyle Dane Bernbach might be counted on to hire Jews, but it was unlikely with the other advertising agencies, and the only Jews who might be hired by *any* advertising agency were from more prestigious schools than mine. I disregarded that. I thought I was different and special and with my resume and my impressive college credentials, the prejudices wouldn't apply to me. My resume didn't state I was a Jewish boy from the Bronx, simply someone from the Bronx. I didn't appreciate in that world, coming from the Bronx meant you came from the Bronx. Madison Avenue wasn't populated with people from the Bronx.

Many years after this, at the home of a friend, I met Phyllis Robinson, a pioneer creative executive in the advertising business and a mainstay at Doyle Dane Bernbach. We talked about that period when I was first looking for a job as an advertising copywriter and she said she never would have hired me. She would not have been favorably disposed to the trade school aspect of my background, that I had actually studied advertising in school and taken advertising copy courses, she told me. She would have preferred an English major who had something unusual about him. This was one person's opinion, but an important creative person in advertising, who said my very choice of school and my course of study was in her view, misguided.

For something I wrote further along in my adult life, I spoke to an employment agency person who had been active in placing people in advertising jobs at the time I had been looking for a job. This person confirmed that anti-Semitism and an old-boy network definitely existed in the advertising agency business then, and those years were extremely unfavorable to someone who did not go to an Ivy League school, or at least a prestigious school. The undergraduate business school at N.Y.U. might have been slightly more prestigious than the undergraduate business school at City College, but possibly not, and not sufficiently so to represent a difference to Madison Avenue.

A few years later, everything began to change. "The Graphic Greeks" with people like George Lois, began to make inroads into the art departments of advertising agencies. Then advertising agencies began to hire more "ethnics," as they were bluntly called, and people like Jerry Della Femina, an Italian-American from Brooklyn, infiltrated the copy departments. Even Della Femina met resistance in his early forays. When he brought his copywriting samples to the J. Walter Thompson advertising agency looking for a job on the Ford Motor Company account, he was told his samples were good, but "they don't want your kind."

Eventually, the "ethnics" were hired not only in the creative departments, but in client relations and management positions. Not in the summer of 1956. I was out there too soon. When the changes came, I was beyond caring. But as the time passed that summer, I cared deeply.

I received a call from an employment agency offering an interview for a job as a junior copywriter with a publisher of trade magazines, Breskin Publications, publishers of *Modern Packaging* magazine and *Modern Plastics* magazine with offices on Madison Avenue and 57th Street. The job was writing ads that would appear in the company's magazines for advertisers who did not have their own advertising agencies. This was hardly an advertising agency job, but it was a job writing advertising copy. Desperate to get started, to be working, when the job was offered, I accepted. By taking this job I had begun to close doors on myself for advertising agency work. But they might not ever have been open.

In August 1956, finally, I was a working man. I traveled to work during rush hour on the subway with the other working people from the Bronx who had jobs downtown. I wore suits and ties to the office. In the winter I bought an overcoat, which was a bit long, and an executive's hat, which was an overstatement. In my coat and my hat, I must have looked like a slightly taller version of Toulouse-Lautrec.

VOTING

The first time I voted I was living in the building at 1695 Grand Concourse. I presumed the voting booths would be located at a school, as had been the case when family members voted in the previous neighborhood. The polling place was listed as a street number for a building. I walked over and found a Board of Elections sign at the outside of the service entrance of an ordinary Bronx apartment house on a side street.

I walked through a dark corridor past garbage cans and turned into a space that was obviously a storage room for the basement area of the building. I entered and in a small room with unfinished brick walls and a naked light bulb hanging by a chain from the ceiling, was the polling place. A single voting booth was in the room. An American flag was affixed to the wall behind it. A uniformed police officer stood guard. Two female election officials sat behind a table. Nobody else was there. A more bare-bones polling place could not have been imaginable. I was checked in, closed the booth curtain behind me and voted. I emerged, the only voter. I nodded, they all nodded, and I walked back out past the garbage cans.

This was not a letdown for my first time voting, to vote in such an inauspicious setting. I thought it was excellent, that a system was set up that would include a room like that with an American flag and people on duty no matter how small the room, because every vote counted, and I had no doubt that my vote that day in the Bronx, my first vote, would be properly tallied.

FULFILLING YOUR MILITARY OBLIGATION

At Breskin Publications I was able to write an advertising campaign that used cartoons as artwork for a company in the plastics industry. The campaign was the closest in its appearance to coveted consumer advertising of any work I did there and nothing like it was going to cross my desk for a while. I could also see that years might pass before I would move up in the office. I decided to leave after a year, a portfolio in hand of sample ads in the real world, and with hopes I could yet break into the world of Madison Avenue advertising agencies.

First, I needed to deal with the Army. I was going for the six months option. A friend from college, Eugene Secunda, told me about an Army Reserve unit he signed up for and recommended that I should, too. The Army Reserve or National Guard unit you joined determined your Army job for the three-plus months on active duty that followed the two months of basic training, and also determined the nature of your weekly meetings and two-week summer assignments during the subsequent six years of your military commitment. This unit was for Army public information. You needed to be qualified to get in. Eugene gave me the name of the Army sergeant to see and I went with a resume and my portfolio—to get into the Army.

The scene in the building on West 42nd Street that was home to the Army Reserve units was a Mack Sennett comedy. Young men in civilian clothes frantic about getting into a unit before they were drafted for two years were racing through the building, up and down stairs, trying to get in somewhere, shouting to each other, "Who has openings?" and on hearing, "Medics," or "Signal Corps," they would race to the office that had the openings.

I walked in to see the sergeant in charge of enlistments for the public information unit. You really did have to qualify with experience in journalism or with related experience. I had written press releases at Breskin Publications about articles that appeared in the magazines and I had written ads. He looked at my resume, thumbed through my portfolio and I was hired. That is to say, he signed me up.

I needed to get my enlistment accelerated, wrote to my Congressman, my papers came through rapidly, and I was sent to Fort Dix, New Jersey. The Korean War was over. This was peacetime, which lent an inessential quality to basic training. My company was a combination of enlistees, draftees, and six months people. We didn't seem to be learning skills that would defeat the enemy and perhaps save our lives, rather skills to get us through basic training. The regular Army training cadre, many of whom had fought in Korea, were putting in their hours and the general idea was to move us along. Basic training was manageable. I did have a mortifying moment during a class on the assembly and disassembly of the M-1 rifle. The sergeant in charge of the class asked the two hundred or so men in the hall seated with rifle parts in front of them to stop whatever they were doing and direct their attention to me. "Never in all my years in this man's Army," he drawled, standing over me, "have I ever seen a soldier attempt to insert the trigger housing group of the M-1 rifle in . . . upside down!" He should have seen my work on the lamp in shop.

In the middle of basic training the custom was to have visitors on a Sunday, rather like parents' visiting day for children at a summer camp. My mother, sister and brother-in-law came and we had a picnic lunch. My brother-in-law, Lenny, was in the Marines during World War II. Like many of his generation, he never talked about the war. Once, I saw his old duffel bag in a closet and on it was written places he had served, including Peleliu, the scene of one of the bloodiest battles of the Pacific Islands. The Army recently had changed its colors from khaki to green. I felt awkward about being in my peacetime, tacky green uniform in his presence. But this was a guy who used to bring me comic books when he was dating my sister. He was not there to make me feel uncomfortable and merely joined in on the day. The people of my time in military service were enormously lucky, serving when we did.

After basic training, the six months soldiers were assigned to work in Army jobs within their Reserve unit's specialty. I received orders to remain at Fort Dix to work in the post public information office. I might have been a civilian employee but for the uniform I wore. My job was writing press releases about Fort Dix activities and personnel. I slept in a barracks with other soldiers who worked at post headquarters. We needed to conform to Army regulations, inspections, KP, we *were* in the Army, but we worked a conventional office work week. I was going to indicate the Army on my next resume for Madison Avenue—to not only show the Army was out of the way, to also boost my writing credentials. That seemed amazing to me, to serve in the Army and for it to somehow be a plus on your resume.

On a hot summer Saturday I returned home from Fort Dix for the weekend. Some of my old friends had left New York for jobs in other cities. A friend from college who lived nearby was not around. I was not dating anyone. I didn't know who I might call or see or what I might do. Although there was a schoolyard nearby, I didn't play schoolyard ball any longer. I could have gone to the movies. I could have done that on post. My mother's move to a more refined section of the Grand Concourse where stores did not occupy the street level had translated itself into streets that were dead in the summer. I no longer had a neighborhood. I only lived in a building.

I did not stay the night and returned to Fort Dix. On succeeding summer weekends, I often elected not to go home. I stayed on post where, temporarily, I belonged.

As a gesture to our men in uniform, movies were made available in the post movie theaters concurrent with their openings in Manhattan. These were single-feature showings, the first at six, the second around eight. I became a movie critic for several people in my barracks. I would usually go to the six o'clock show for the latest new movie, return to the barracks where my Army buddies would be napping. They would peer at me through half-open eyes when I came in and if I nodded, yes, they would get out of their bunks and go to the movie, and if I shook my head, no, they would go back to sleep. This was being a powerful critic.

ONCE MORE

Breskin Publications went to the top of my resume. I placed the Army ahead of college. No more ads in my portfolio from college classes or from a college newspaper. I had samples to show of ads that appeared in print in the business world. I re-registered with employment agencies, sent my resume to advertising agencies, and scanned the classifieds. Once more, I couldn't get a job with an advertising agency.

I was at a pivotal moment, not knowing whether to keep trying or accept the situation and take the best non-advertising agency job that came along. In a newspaper article about the specialization of advertising agencies, this joke was cited: "Someone goes out for a job and is asked, 'Any experience with consumer advertising?' 'Yes.' 'Packaged goods?' 'Yes.' 'Cigarettes?' 'Yes.' 'Filter-tip or regular?' " In that specialized field, if I took another job in anything other than an advertising agency I would label myself as someone who had been unable after college to compile any advertising agency experience. A second job not with an advertising agency would be decisive, in my judgment, and I would never get in. As the months of trying for work in an advertising agency built up and I still couldn't get hired, the message was clear, I wasn't getting in—and I needed a job.

An employment agency person recommended I apply for a job that was open with Ziff Davis magazines in the sales promotion department. He said these were consumer magazines—*Popular Photography* and *Car and Driver* among them—and working there would be an improvement over my previous experience with a trade magazine publisher. He told me it was creative work and there was a career to be made working in magazine sales promotion. I understood the implications of a job like that. My hopes of being an advertising agency copywriter would be over. After a series of interviews, I was offered a job there and I accepted.

I worked as a writer of sales promotion material and scripts for sales presentations to help the salesmen sell advertising space in the various Ziff Davis magazines. The department consisted of a director, manager, two writers senior to me, another writer on my level, and myself. All but one were Jewish. Evidently, magazine sales promotion was where Jews who couldn't get into advertising agencies settled.

The one non-Jewish person in the department was Greek-American, Stanley Anton, a fine copywriter, but the hiring of "ethnics" at advertising agencies hadn't come to pass when he started his work life and he was working where he had been able to get hired.

Years later, one of my colleagues from that department, Ken Silverbush, said to me, "Of all of us, you were the most aware there was another advertising world out there, the real advertising world, and we weren't in it." I was probably good at it, while being acutely aware of the other advertising world out there that I wasn't in.

If you could only see ahead and be able to say to yourself, it's going to be all right. Working in a job where you write trade magazine ads will lead to a job where you'll write scripts for sales presentations and writing them will enable you to get work writing scripts for educational films. And with that as an economic support, you'll be able to try being a writer one day. So don't beat yourself up so badly. Being an advertising agency copywriter isn't crucial. You thought it was what you needed to overcome your family background, but you're going to be doing something entirely different from what you thought you needed to do. If you could only see ahead.

LEAVING

I had written the parodies of songs as a camp counselor and it occurred to me to try writing lyrics for real songs. I knew a couple of people who had aspirations to write music and I collaborated with them. I sometimes wrote lyrics on the subway going between the Bronx and my job with Ziff Davis in Manhattan. Nothing ever happened with these songs, but an idea was taking shape, that there were other kinds of writing I could try.

I began seeing a sophisticated young woman who lived in the next building on the Grand Concourse, Sandy Resnick, who worked in fashion and was a fan of Mabel Mercer and Bobby Short. I was living with a less sophisticated songbook, someone still in the Bronx in an apartment he shared with his mother. In other words, my living arrangement was increasingly unacceptable.

Then came the polar bears girl, she of "If you had your own apartment we could go there now." I quickly determined I had saved enough money to get my own apartment in Manhattan. In February 1960, I rented an apartment on East

31st Street, a few blocks from the office building where I worked. I was more relieved by the move than exultant. I took my clothing and some books and I left the Bronx.

About a year later, I was fired from Ziff Davis in an economic slowdown. Each department was required to let someone go. I was the youngest and the only single man in the department, and my being fired was presented to me as management being humanitarian in behalf of the older, married men.

In the Army Reserve unit I had become friendly with Herb Gardner who, in his twenties, had written the Broadway hit, *A Thousand Clowns*. As was our custom, after our weekly Reserve meeting, we went to eat in a Times Square delicatessen. I said to him, somewhat awkwardly, that I was thinking of becoming a writer. He told me I shouldn't be so tentative about it. "I can see the way you observe things, the way you express yourself, you can be a writer. Just don't make it into a science fiction movie. I've got a Broadway play on a few blocks away. These things can happen, but they won't happen if you make it into science fiction. I know you. You can do it."

A while later, I was walking through Washington Square Park with Paul Krassner, the publisher of *The Realist*, a popular underground magazine of the time. I had come to know him through a person who worked at Ziff Davis. I did a comic riff about dating as we walked along and he was laughing. He said that if I wrote it up just the way I said it, he would publish it in *The Realist*. A few days later he called and said, "Where's my piece?" I wrote it and he published it, my first article in print. He went on to publish several other things of mine. Soon after the first appeared, Herb Gardner said to me, "I saw your article in *The Realist*. I am so proud of you."

Any miscalculations I might have made in trying to become

an advertising agency copywriter, and any prejudices that might have blocked my path, had become irrelevant. They were part of an obsolete dream. I watched foreign films when I was a little boy. I was always good at English in school. Did I have to make a career in business? I turned away from business writing. I found a good way of paying my bills, writing free-lance scripts for an educational film company while I tried to become a full-time writer. I wrote a couple of plays that went unproduced and magazine articles that were published. Then I wrote a novel without a contract, hoping to find a publisher. It was *Oh, God!* The first publisher I submitted it to accepted it. A successful movie was made of it. I went on to write the novel, *Kramer vs. Kramer.* A full-time writer is what I had become.

In 1988, I was asked to contribute an article for a *New York Times Magazine* supplement on the the subject of neighborhoods of the city. This is what I wrote:

In the summer of 1955, when I was 19 and the Grand Concourse was in bloom in every respect, I decided to take a walk in my newly purchased Bermuda shorts. These were the earliest days for Bermudas; they were seldom seen on the streets of the city, and you wore them with high argyle socks. I was striding along the Concourse when a middle-aged woman stepped in my path, glared at my bare knees and proclaimed, "You're a disgrace to the Bronx!"

The Bronx was a place people took pride in, especially the Grand Concourse, the wide, tree-lined street where the "better" buildings were found, "the Park Avenue of the Bronx," or as one of the regulars might have said, "a regular Champs-Elysées." For generations of people, the Concourse was not only *the* street where Bronxites aspired to live, it was also a social and cultural attraction. Like the successful malls of today—the Galleria in Houston, for instance—it was a gathering place for strolling, shopping, eating, movies.

A few years ago I wrote a novel called *The Old Neighborhood*, in which the main character, rootless and distraught, returns to his childhood neighborhood near the Grand Concourse to find himself. Since then, it has been intriguing to me the way readers have made personal connections to that book, writing to me about it, telling me what it meant to them. Something about the Bronx and the Grand Concourse area has a powerful emotional hold on people.

Part of it has to do, I think, with a sense of loss. The culture in which we grew up there has vanished. In the 1960's and

1970's urban blight swept across the Bronx with such ferocity that its burned, abandoned housing looked like pictures we have seen of London during the blitz. The expression "South Bronx" became synonymous with inner-city disintegration, and what was regarded as the South Bronx moved inexorably north to include much of what been the central part of the borough.

Another reason for people's connection to the place, and my own, I suspect, is the way we romanticize our childhood. For people now middle-aged, the years in the 1940's and 1950's were clearly simpler, more innocent times. But there was something undeniably special about those old Bronx neighborhoods—the tumult, the colorfulness and, especially, the sense of community—which many of us miss today.

I have gone back to look around the Bronx many times, out of nostalgia, curiosity, concern for the area where I grew up. Recently, realtors and civic groups have been talking about a revival of the Bronx and the Concourse area, and so I went back once again to see what was happening there. Walking along the streets, inevitably, I remembered what the area was like when I was growing up. Every neighborhood was linked culturally and geographically to the Grand Concourse, running for over four miles through the heart of the borough.

The Concourse and Fordham Road constituted the main commercial hub of the Bronx, with Alexander's department store at its crossroads, retail stores spread out on all sides. You could get a charlotte russe with fresh whipped cream at a frozen custard stand opposite Alexander's, on the south side of Fordham Road, or an egg cream in the candy store just off the Concourse on 188th Street, a bookies' and bettors' hangout. (Incidentally, for an egg cream, if you put the milk in first, then the soda and the chocolate syrup last, you get a beautiful-looking dark drink with a perfect white, foamy head. But given the passions of egg cream experts, I haven't heard the last on that subject.)

Loew's Paradise was on the Concourse south of 188th Street, that huge, eccentrically baroque movie palace, with nymphs adorning the walls of the theater beneath the stars and moving clouds on the ceiling. Across the street from the Paradise was Krum's, the quintessential soda parlor, and in those simpler times you sat at counter with a date and didn't consider it déclassé.

If you wanted to be "intellectual," a few blocks south, on the Concourse and 183rd Street, was the Ascot Theater, one of the first art movie houses in New York. *Open City, The Bicycle Thief,* the Marcel Pagnol *Fanny* trilogy all played there when they were first released in this country.

The Concourse was where you promenaded in your best clothes on the Jewish holidays and on Easter Sunday. The true boulevardiers never spent much time in a synagogue or a church on those days, they just checked out the action.

During World War II, the Concourse was the scene of big parades on Memorial Day, and when the war ended people crowded along the parade route to cheer the returning servicemen from their neighborhoods.

And the Concourse was where you strolled, just strolled, with friends at night—"Walk me for a soda." On a recent return trip, I take the IRT No. 4 train uptown to the Bedford Park Boulevard stop, which is in the Concourse's northern section. This area now probably has the highest percentage of white residents of any part of the Grand Concourse region; farther south the proportions change, and the neighborhoods are predominantly Hispanic and black. Favored by geography, with the New York Botanical Garden on the east and the Jerome Park reservoir on the west, the northern Concourse is an area with low-density population and a limited amount of housing that could have become blighted. It looks much as I remember it did in the 1940's.

Near Kingsbridge Road, I pass a scene that makes me smile. A few feet from a sign that says "Positively no ball playing allowed," a group of Asian youngsters are batting around a ball, just as we would have done in our day.

Apart from a fenced area protecting the Edgar Allan Poe cottage, which has been restored and maintained, sadly, Poe Park is filthy, the grass, what there is of it, burned out; I assume that either people have recently been abusing this place with litter and soda and beer cans, or it hasn't been cleaned properly in weeks.

I pass Alexander's department store. The Fordham Road-Grand Concourse section of retail stores is clearly still a viable shopping area. The streets are crowded with shoppers, mostly black and Hispanic. You see few empty stores here; the businesses are similar to those you would find along 34th Street or 86th Street in Manhattan, stores selling clothing, shoes, electronics. Some of the chains are here—Seaman's, Radio Shack, Kleinsleep, Trader Horn, Newmark & Lewis. The Loew's Paradise has been subdivided, so to speak, and is now four theaters; young people are standing in line.

I am now approaching the street where I once lived, and as I walk on I realize that the highway signs I first noticed farther north, which I took to be somehow necessary because streets like Fordham Road are major thoroughfares, continue all along the Concourse. They are exit signs, and some of the exit signs they point to are ludicrous—small side streets. They are not little signs, either; they are nearly the size of the signs on the Long Island Expressway. Later, I learned that they were

placed along the Grand Concourse several years ago in order
to aid motorists. Aid motorists? These large, hideous signs
announce to everyone walking along the Concourse, or living
there: Don't deceive yourself into thinking this is a street for
people any longer. This is a highway and don't you forget it.

I lived in an apartment whose windows faced the Grand
Concourse, on Field Place, between 183rd and 184th Streets,
a five-story red brick walk-up with a white facade entrance,
retail stores on the street level. The red brick has become
sorely darkened with time and the white facade has faded.
Fisher's candy store used to be on the corner. It was a slightly
higher-level operation than most Bronx candy stores in that
it featured an active lunch counter. It also sold a house specialty that I have never seen since—a "frozen malted," ice
milk served soft in cups and cones. Fisher's is now El Tropi-
cal Cuchifritos Restaurant.

At the entrance to our building is a step where I would
sit and read or daydream. I sit down again on my childhood
stoop, facing the street where I remember belly-whopping
down a hill with abandon after a snow. Seen through my
adult eyes, the hill is merely a slight downgrade. I am so
flooded with memories and with a sense of the passage of
time that I simply cannot handle sitting there for more than
a minute. I move on.

The Ascot Theater is now a porno house. But at East Mt.
Eden Avenue, Bronx-Lebanon Hospital is being expanded
with a new building facing the Grand Concourse. A sign at
the site proclaims, "The Bronx is rebuilding its future with
pride." South of 170th Street, the last five vacant buildings
on the Concourse were recently turned over to private devel-
opers for rehabilitation, and work on them has begun. Since
1981, more than $120 million from Federal, city and private

funds has been invested in restoring over 150 buildings on the Concourse and, to a lesser extent, adjacent streets.

Facing the entrance of Public School 64 on Walton Avenue and East 171st Street, there is a gutted, abandoned apartment house. This is the sight children have had to see every day on their way to school. But a sign has just gone up announcing that the building is being rehabilitated.

As I continue along the Concourse to 161st Street, and walk the side streets, I notice very real examples of urban renewal. The area is certainly looking better than when I came through here several years ago. The place was so run-down then it was almost unbearable to see.

Perhaps because I have written about the Bronx, I have become a kind of Bronxologist. I am often asked by people who also lived there—What happened? We moved away, and a few years later we were reading about massive blighted areas.

What happened in the Bronx was replicated in many of the inner cities across the country. Tremendous shifts in population during and after World War II changed the nature of city neighborhoods. But the decline of the Bronx was particularly rapid and vast.

During the 1930's and then in the 1940's, when I was growing up there, the Grand Concourse and its side streets were a magnet for people from the Lower East Side of Manhattan and from the east Bronx. The newcomers were predominantly Jewish, but there was, too, a large Irish-Catholic population. The neighborhoods linked to the Concourse were white and, by the standards of those years, middle class.

After the war, rural Southern blacks poured into Northern cities in search of factory jobs. In New York they were joined by large numbers of Puerto Ricans, many with poor English-language skills. Settling in Harlem and East Harlem, this new population eventually filtered into the southeast Bronx. Meanwhile, people in the Bronx were moving from the east Bronx to the Grand Concourse area, from the Concourse to Queens or to the suburbs. We all knew people who were leaving; they were "the rich kids." For young couples the old neighborhood was beginning to feel old. Home ownership beckoned in the new communities on Long Island and New Jersey, and many found it culturally unacceptable to live near their parents.

As blacks and Hispanics began moving into Bronx neighborhoods, many whites began to retreat in white flight. Bluntly, part of what some whites of my generation and older are nostalgic about concerning the Bronx is the fact that they were able to live under apartheid right here in New York City.

The postwar relocations had to change the character of Bronx neighborhoods. But couldn't these areas have remained relatively as stable and as racially mixed as the northern Concourse is today? I asked Robert Caro, who wrote the highly praised biography of Robert Moses, *The Power Broker*, if he thought the deterioration that took place in the Bronx was inevitable, given those geographical shifts in the population of the city that had resulted in shifts in economic levels. "Not necessarily," he said. "The farther away you get from the Cross Bronx Expressway, the more stable the neighborhoods are."

It was the building of the Cross Bronx Expressway and the construction of Co-op City that accelerated the decline of the Bronx.

In 1945, Robert Moses, wanting to link the George Washington Bridge to the Bronx Whitestone Bridge, received permission from city officials to build a major roadway and for the next 10 years proceeded to smash a six-lane highway across seven miles of the Bronx, devastating neighborhood after neighborhood, scattering populations, tipping poorer neighborhoods into slums that were inhabited by the economically insolvent, creating chaos.

To really see the Cross Bronx Expressway you have to be at a stationary vantage point, not in a car. I stood at 174th Street and the Grand Concourse. From that high point, the arrogance is palpable. From east and west there is a continuous flood of trucks and cars. The huge, ugly tongue that is this highway seems to spite not only the immediate area that was leveled, but everything within its vicinity.

The Expressway accelerated the pace of existing changes in the population of the south and east Bronx. More and more low-income blacks and Hispanics moved into the newly created slums. Whites continued to leave the west Bronx and Concourse area out of upward mobility or out of white flight. And then Co-op City opened its doors.

Built on the site of Freedom Land, a defunct amusement park in the far reaches of the northeast Bronx, this monolithic cluster of high-rises opened in December 1968. More than 15,000 apartments were made available for purchase at very inexpensive prices, and by the thousands whites evacuated the Concourse and other areas of the Bronx to live there. It was the final bell.

When I told people that I intended to go back to the Bronx to look around, they were concerned about my safety—Don't be up there after dark. I went uptown several times, walking for miles along the Grand Concourse and its adjacent streets. The walks extended into nighttime, yet I never felt in any danger. One tough-looking youth fixed me with a hard stare as I walked past him. I took it to be an expression he cultivated for all outsiders. I imagined him working on it in front of a mirror. Two flashily dressed men driving a convertible stopped the car and leaped out to have an intense conversation with a man in a doorway who then rushed into the car with them, and they drove away. I had the distinct impression that I should not go up to them and say, "Excuse me, I'm doing some research. Might I enquire as to the specific nature of the business you are conducting here?"

That was it. Nobody took notice of me. The streets were busy with the city life of a pleasant evening: children playing, street-corner conversations, parents strolling with infants.

As someone who grew up in the Grand Concourse area, and who was told his Bermuda shorts were a disgrace to the Bronx, I found walking through it now frustrating, perplexing. I would pass an abandoned building or a vacant lot and nearby would be a recently restored building, with well-dressed people on their way in and out.

I eventually concluded that the realtors and civic leaders are, to a certain extent, right: there is a sense of renewal in the Bronx. Neighborhoods that were once middle-class and white and became blighted now have the chance of becoming middle-class again and racially mixed. But I know what this place looked like years ago, and the parks today are still too littered, the streets are still too dirty, there are too many abandoned buildings still standing. The only way this situation can change is through the pride of the people living there, a pride that can be helped along by a sense of the commitment of public officials. As a small start, those damn highway signs, which shouldn't be there at all, could be taken down overnight with the same kind of edict that ignored the community and put them up in the first place.

One scene from my trips uptown stays with me. A group of young Hispanic girls are playing on a sidewalk. They are singing and skipping to *London Bridge is Falling Down*, forming arches with their arms, slipping under, singing the song in soft accents. They are so beautiful, the moment is so pure and lovely that it stops me in my tracks. It is possible that these children will grow up in a neighborhood clean and stable, and feeling good about themselves for that; one day they will move up and out as previous generations have done. Or perhaps their children will. For that to happen the Concourse area has to be a kind of model city within the city. It has to be valued by Government so that every effort is made to keep those streets clean and safe.

"The Bronx is rebuilding its future with pride." One hopes. In 1988, the Grand Concourse area is at a tipping point as crucial as the one in the late 1960's when the area unraveled. The progress of these last years will continue, or it will all slide back.

You can take the boy out of the Bronx, but you can't take the Bronx out of the boy, and I am still rooting for the place.

What's Happening On The Street Of Dreams
The New York Times, November 20, 1988.

Since I wrote that piece, I still root for the place, and the tipping point has passed—with the Bronx on the positive side. The progress has continued.

After the 50th anniversary of our 6th grade graduation, Richard Kobliner, who had told me about that gathering, said he was going to try convening some of the people not specifically from our 6th grade, other people from our neighborhood. He was only partially successful; we were a small group. I came, as did Richard, and two people I barely knew while growing up, but one of my good friends from the neighborhood was there. We reminisced over dinner in a Manhattan restaurant. As we were leaving, I stood apart from the others with my old friend, Bobby, who had become Robert C. Grogin, professor of history at the University of Saskatchewan. My remark to him, the fact that I would even say it, indicated how much my family history and my profound embarrassment about it were a part of me back then, and still in my emotional DNA. "Children can be known to be cruel," I said, "but I can't remember a single time anyone out of anger threw up to me that my parents were divorced and that I lived in a household of deaf-mutes." His response went to the heart of the sense of community we all shared in those years and how much we meant to each other. "It would have been," he said, "unthinkable."